GAS BARBECUING

*The new way of outdoor cooking
– a complete guide*

JIM MARKS

MARTIN BOOKS

NOTES ON RECIPES

Ingredients are given in both metric and imperial measures. Use either set of quantities, but not a mixture of both, in any one recipe.

All spoon measurements are level unless otherwise stated:

1 tablespoon = one 15 ml spoon;

1 teaspoon = one 5 ml spoon.

Eggs are standard (size three) unless otherwise stated.

Published by Martin Books
Simon & Schuster Consumer Group
Fitzwilliam House
32 Trumpington Street
Cambridge CB2 1QY

First published 1990
Second impression 1991

Text © Jim Marks, 1990, 1991
Photographs and illustrations © Woodhead-Faulkner
(Publishers) Ltd, 1990, 1991

ISBN 0 85941 618 6

Design: Carrods Graphic Design, Cambridge
Photography: Geoff Stanton Photography
Food preparation for photography: Jim Marks and
Susan Williams
Illustrations: Carrods Graphic Design, Cambridge
Typesetting: Goodfellow & Egan Ltd, Cambridge
Printed and bound in Great Britain by
BPCC Hazell Books,
Aylesbury

Cover dishes: Grilled red mullet with fennel (page 97); Steak au poivre flambé (page 47); Chicken with chilli glaze (page 82); Mixed vegetable kebabs (page 106), Prawn and vegetable kebabs (page 43), Beef and courgette kebabs (page 55); Sweet and sour pork (page 73)

Contents

Index

Acknowledgements

Once again my wife Brenda has met and conquered the challenge of deciphering my barely legible scribblings and transmitted them on to paper. My sincere thanks for this and also for her kind help with all the hard work that writing the book entailed.

I have long admired the expertise of my friend Geoff Stanton and would like to thank him and his skilful colleague, Tracey Sherwood, for their dedicated efforts which resulted in the lovely photographs in this book. My thanks to Susan Williams in providing expert assistance with the food presentation, and also to my editor, Jessica Williams, for her gentle persuasion in ensuring that my nose was kept to the grindstone.

I would also like to take this opportunity to thank my friends at Calor Gas Limited for their kind assistance in providing equipment for photography, and technical advice, and also to express my thanks to the many manufacturers and distributors of gas barbecues who have done likewise.

Finally, my thanks to McCormick Foods for kindly providing the information used in the herb and spice chart on pages 135–9.

Jim Marks is known as 'Mr Barbecue' and is widely regarded as Britain's leading barbecue specialist. His knowledge and expertise has led to his participation in many radio phone-ins and he has appeared frequently on television, including BBC 2's 'Food and Drink' programme. He has also had several books and articles published, including Barbecues and Better Barbecuing. His international reputation means that he is in great demand for lectures and seminars, and he has given hundreds of live barbecue demonstrations both at home and abroad.

Introduction

Having spent a lot of time and effort over the past twenty years preaching and teaching the joys of barbecuing to the public, I am greatly pleased that this uniquely American import – surely one of the best – has taken firm root in Britain. It is no longer a tender plant that thrives only when the sun shines, although growth has naturally been most vigorous when summers are fine and warm.

Judging from the people I have had the pleasure of chatting to during my barbecue demonstrations, there are many who use their barbecues all year round and don't stow them away at the first hint of autumn. There have always been enthusiasts who use their barbecues come rain or shine, but doing so only became a practical proposition with the advent of the covered gas barbecue. Having conducted hundreds of gas-barbecue cook-outs at agricultural shows, exhibitions, and the like during the past few years (involving a total cooking time of over 2,000 hours), I can say that neither gale-force wind, torrential rain nor snow has ever prevented the barbecue from doing its stuff. However, it is not just the ease of lighting, fast warm-up and precise heat control in all weather conditions that makes a gas barbecue such a joy to use, it is also the marvellous results that can be achieved with surprisingly little effort and without even modest culinary skill.

My hope is that you will be tempted to work your way through the recipe section; my regret is that I will not be there when you open the lid of your gas barbecue and reveal a mouth-watering roast, an apple pie or, for that special occasion, perhaps a magnificent Boeuf en Croûte! Whatever the event, please accept my very best wishes for your future 'gastronomic' endeavours.

Happy barbecuing and bon appetit.

Choosing your equipment

If you happen to be the proud owner of a gas barbecue, I suggest you skip this section and move on to Parts Two, Three and Four. However, for those who are contemplating buying their first gas-fired barbecue, time spent browsing through this section could well pay dividends. It sometimes happens that following the purchase and initial use of an expensive household, garden or sporting item, it turns out to be lacking a really useful accessory or feature, or is too small or too cumbersome for the task selected.

This section is not intended to be a 'best buy' report, although I will occasionally state my preference for a particular feature or a particular barbecue accessory. In any case, a thorough practical test of the 150 or so gas barbecues currently available in this country would require several summers, many tons of food and lots of stamina! While it is nice to have such a choice it could make your task more difficult. It is therefore sensible to consider the basic factors affecting your choice before going shopping. Bear in mind that the retail prices of washing machines and, of greater relevance, free-standing cookers, relate very closely to the retail prices of gas barbecues, and decide on the price you are prepared to pay. Then work out how big the unit's cooking area (capacity) needs to be to cope with your *normal* catering demands. Consider the various design options covered in the chapter dealing with your choice of model in conjunction with the manufacturers' sales literature.

Gas barbecues are not the rare animals they were, so you may have practitioners of this form of barbecuing among your friends and acquaintances. If they are typical of the gas-barbecuing fraternity they will be glad to give you the benefit of their experience. Unbiased advice of this kind is invaluable in helping you to gauge the suitability of a particular barbecue. Ask about overall efficiency, capability in handling the demands of the number of your guests and durability.

As far as I am concerned, the most important factor when choosing a gas barbecue that is destined to spend its life on the patio, is that it should have twin burners. Nowadays, I'm glad to say, most patio units (and in particular the 'wagons') do. The reasons for making this my priority are quite straightforward.

Firstly, shutting off one of the two burners enables you to use the barbecue for more than simple grilling of flat meats and fish, because it can then be used for roasting, baking and smoke-cooking (see Part Three).

Secondly, one can vary, at will, the temperature of each half of the cooking area, which makes it perfect for cooking lots of steaks to varying degrees.

Thirdly, energy and money are saved when cooking a small quantity of food (which will probably be most of the time) because just one burner and one half of the cooking area is used – not the entire area as in a single burner unit.

Before visiting your local source of supply – be it a specialist dealer handling bottled gas and allied equipment, garden centre, hardware store or departmental store – I suggest you make the following list of check-points. This might be useful when choosing betwen two or more units which are similar in size and price.
○ Check if the barbecue has been passed by the Calor Gas Laboratories (BS 5258) or has the approval of the American Gas Association (AGA) or the Canadian Gas Association (CGA). AGA and CGA approved barbecues will have a sticker on the unit. However, not all Calor Gas approved units sport a distinctive badge, so if in doubt,

check with the retailer.

○ Check the power rating: expressed in British Thermal Units (BTUs) or kilowatts. As a rough guide, divide the total BTUs by the size of the cooking area (in square inches). An ideal rating would be around 100 BTUs per square inch.

○ Check if the barbecue has an approved regulator; this regulates the high pressure flow of gas from the cylinder to the burners. Most units will be supplied with a gas regulator but, if not, a specialist dealer in bottled gas will be able to advise on, and supply, the correct item (see below).

○ Check if sufficient volcanic (lava) rock is provided with the unit. Ideally there should be enough rock to completely cover the fire-grate in a crowded single layer. A small gap around the perimeter of the grate is acceptable, but largish gaps in the rock layer above the burner would allow some fat to fall on to it and, probably, create a flare-up.

○ Check if the burner controls are in a convenient position for you.

○ Check if the barbecue has a push-button spark igniter (a feature not found on many small, fully portable, gas barbecues).

○ Check if wheeled barbecues are relatively easy to manoeuvre. But remember, *never attempt to move a barbecue when the burner is alight*.

○ Check if the barbecue has a warming grill. The more generously sized the warming grill the better – ideally around fifty per cent of the main cooking grill area. (A unit with a large warming grill could perhaps enable you to trade down to a slightly smaller barbecue.)

○ Check the position of the lid handle. One on the front of the lid could mean your wrist and lower arm are exposed to the heat whilst lifting and closing the lid. (If the handle on the lid is at the front, it is very important that the cook wears a good quality gauntlet – a long glove that covers the lower forearm as well as the hand.)

○ Check that the rotisserie spit rod (if supplied) is sturdy: it should be able to support a decent-sized joint or a couple of chickens without deflecting unduly. The thumbscrews securing the meat tines to the rod should be able to stand regular tightening (perhaps with pliers) without the threads stripping.

Note: most gas barbecues are made to accommodate a spit roast assembly. However, if you will be getting one, check that the barbecue's bottom casting includes the necessary fixing holes.

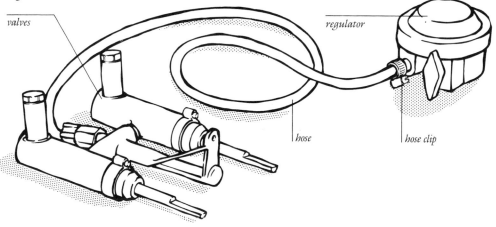

Regulator assembly – quick-coupling type (designs may vary)

○ Check that the barbecue lid fits neatly and is not distorted anywhere.

○ Check the barbecue's stability by giving it a nudge. Excessive wobbling in a display barbecue could be caused by poor assembly or because the supporting frame's nuts and bolts have become loose through being moved around.

Portable (table top) gas barbecues

This is the ideal barbecue for taking in the car boot to your holiday destination – especially if it is a self-catering one – whether the accommodation is a caravan, tent, house or boat.

There is relatively little difference in size and shape between competing makes of these compact barbecues (cooking areas average around 150 square inches/967 square cm). They all operate off a single 'ribbon' burner (a straight and narrow burner). The power can, however, vary quite considerably, ranging from 10,000 BTUs (2.9 kilowatts) to 20,000 BTUs (5.8 kilowatts). There are two categories of power source available:

(a) self-sealing butane gas cartridges;
(b) standard (re-fillable) butane gas cylinders, such as Calor Gas.

Fully portable gas barbecues

Those models powered by a gas cartridge can be classified as 'fully portable' because the combined weight of barbecue and cartridge could be as little as 6 kg (13 lb), thus making the trek to the beach or river bank a possibility.

Apart from being very lightweight the cartridge has one other great advantage – its general availability throughout Western Europe. Its main drawback, however, is its short life when compared to the larger re-fillable cylinders. A 300 g (10½ oz) butane cartridge will last for approximately one and a half hours, and that burning time could be considerably reduced if the air temperature is low and the wind strong (more information on this in Part Four). Another factor which could affect the lasting power of the cartridge is the injudicious use of the high heat setting. It is true to say, however, that given reasonable weather and light-handed use, a new cartridge should cope with the normal cooking requirements for a family picnic (or even two or three such events). It is still prudent, though, to take a spare cartridge – just in case.

One of the cartridge-powered units currently available can be adapted, if required, to run off refillable butane gas containers, thus making it considerably more economical to use.

Portable gas barbecues

If it's not your intention to wander off the beaten track but to confine your barbecue cook-outs to the caravan/camp site or to the back garden then it would make sense – economically – to select a unit which operates solely off a standard butane gas cylinder. For many people, particularly caravanners, this will allow greater use of a cylinder already doing duty with a cooker or room heater. Operating a gas barbecue from a refillable cylinder is very economical when compared to running the same unit from a small cartridge, but the cost of running a small 'cartridge barbecue' can compare favourably to a charcoal-burning alternative.

Some portable units incorporate a metal tray to give support to the barbecue's fold-up legs or to act as a warming tray. A metal tray also helps to protect table surfaces from the heat radiating from the base of the burner housing.

One particular portable model, complete with warming tray, has its own wheeled cart in which it sits firmly at a good working height when being used at home. By using the handle, the barbecue can be lifted out of the cart when necessary without the need to undo any nuts and bolts.

Needless to say, all truly portable barbecues have a carrying handle which is usually formed by the folded legs.

Most people will probably be content to use their portable gas barbecue for rustling up a few steaks, burgers or whole fish (particularly if it is their second barbecue chosen for holiday and picnic use). In this case, a basic 'open' unit will suffice, although a covered (lidded) unit would nevertheless help to keep cats and dogs away from a food-encrusted grill.

However, for those wishing occasionally to try their hand at cooking a small chicken, a small roast or an apple pie, the barbecue should have a lid (the deeper the better). Both the lid and lower housing should be of good quality *cast* metal construction. A portable gas barbecue constructed from *sheet* metal should never be used for 'lid-on' cooking, as the lid would quickly warp and the enamel coating flake off on to the food. (See page 33 for tips on using a small portable gas barbecue for roasting and baking.)

One particular model, worthy of mention, can be used for cooking small joints and, when the lid is down and the gas lit, the polished aluminium surface of the lid acts as a griddle. The lid also incorporates a drain channel and drain holes to take care of the fat falling from bacon and burgers. Apart from griddling flat meats, and frying eggs, the lid can also be used for making pancakes and scones.

Semi-portable (pedestal) gas barbecues

The phrase 'semi-portable' is meant to indicate barbecues which will stand in the back garden, or whatever, but could, with the aid of a spanner and a little effort, be fairly quickly taken apart for holidays away from home.

The cooking area of the smaller semi-portable units is, generally speaking, very similar to that of the portable units. The main difference between the two is that the cooking surface of the semi-portable barbecue is set at a good working height.

To qualify as a semi-portable unit the barbecue should, once taken apart, fit into the boot of a typical family saloon car. It follows, therefore, that the barbecue should be of the 'pedestal' variety where the upper housing fits on top of a single column. From experience, I would not recommend taking apart a 'wagon' gas barbecue – not only because of the damage that would probably occur, but because it is still difficult to fit the frame and barbecue housing into the car boot. A 'wagon' incorporating one, or even two, side tables makes the task even more difficult.

Just a year or two ago most gas barbecues for patio entertainment had pedestals. That has now changed to the point where some major manufacturers have dropped pedestal units completely from their ranges. Therefore, if you do want a 'home and away' barbecue, other than one of the portable units, you may have to shop around.

I have already mentioned the benefit of tending food positioned at a comfortable working height, but equally important, in my view, is the siting of the gas control knobs. Most pedestal units have the control knob(s) and push-button igniters positioned part-way down the column, which means a certain amount of bending while cooking. Much easier to operate and control are those pedestal gas barbecues which have the control knob(s) and igniter set into a panel at the front of the burner housing.

A side table is a very useful feature to have on any barbecue, but for these units it is better if it is a clip-on type. Clip-on tables can be purchased from many retail outlets as a standard barbecue accessory.

Another useful feature – worth its weight in gold when having to cope with more food than usual – is a warming grill (sometimes called a warming rack). Most pedestal gas barbecues (apart from some basic, bottom-of-the-range units) have one and for those that do not, it is possible to buy one from good barbecue retailers.

Given adequate tender loving care a gas barbecue should last for many years. One of the first components to show signs of wear is the food grill. Most portable units have chrome-plated wire grills, but the semi-portable units offer a fairly wide choice: chrome-plated, porcelain-coated and stainless steel. If the food grill is chrome-plated, it should have a substantial feel when it is picked up, and not be reminiscent of the bars of a budgie cage. The best grills are triple-nickel-chrome-plated, but, unless so informed, you will have to use your judgement about the quality of the chrome-plating. The bars should be close enough together to prevent small sausages falling through.

Barbecue food grills are increasingly being coated in porcelain. Although it will chip if it is dropped (it should comfortably withstand the impact of an overcooked, rock-hard banger thrown by an exasperated cook!), porcelain is considered to be a superior coating to chrome. It is easier to clean and will stand up better to the occasional scouring.

Some of the less expensive semi-portable units might have a porcelain-coated wire grill. The more expensive models are quite likely to have porcelain-covered steel grills, whilst the top-of-the-range models invariably have porcelain-coated (or porcelainised) cast-iron grills. Cast-iron grills are considered superior because they hold and conduct the heat better than their steel counterparts. As a rule of thumb, the wider the grill bars the better. The inverted U-shape porcelain-coated steel bars are usually around 1 cm (½ inch) wide, whilst the width of the porcelain-coated cast-iron grill bars can be up to 2 cm (¾ inch). One particular gas barbecue I have used quite extensively, has a cast-iron grill with wide bars that are concave in section and slope gently from front to rear. The bars, roughly 2 cm (¾ inch) wide with a 1 cm (½-inch) gap between, catch a good proportion of the fats and juices falling from the food and channel these to the rear edge of the grill.

Wagon gas barbecues

There is no doubt that the name 'wagon' was borrowed from that essential component of wild west movies – the 'chuck-wagon'. A familiar scene from countless westerns is an actor such as John Wayne getting his teeth into a slab of Texan beef barbecued for him by the chuck-wagon cook. (The word 'barbecue' itself preceded the legendary cattle drives by well over a century.)

The major difference between the cowboys' wagon and the modern urban version is that whereas the horse-drawn wagon wandered the plains at will, the gas-fired version is permanently confined to the 'corral' – the back garden patio! For this reason the wagon gas barbecue is sometimes referred to as a patio barbecue.

The weight of the wagon dictates that it is mounted on a wheeled base – generally two large wheels, though exceptionally heavy units usually have an extra pair of swivelling castor wheels to assist pushing and manoeuvring.

The majority of the models on the market have cast aluminium lids and burner housings, although the housings of a few are constructed from sheet steel.

One wagon gas barbecue looks very much like another, especially as far as the hinged box-shaped housing is concerned. There are, however, several useful variations (some listed below), which you should consider before choosing one particular model.

Twin burners

Wagon gas barbecues have individually controlled twin burners (usually made from stainless steel). Depending upon the make and model, the combined burner output can range from 25,000 BTUs (7.3 kilowatts) to 44,000 BTUs (13 kilowatts). Their benefits are outlined on page 10. However, the following comments should help you to select a wagon unit from two or three competing, but not too dissimilar, models, that suit your pocket and the usual weather conditions in your back-yard.

In cold or windy weather, cooking will take longer on a barbecue, especially with the lid open. The combination of stiff breeze and low air temperature can have a dramatic effect – perhaps increasing the cooking time by a factor of two or three (see also page 41 for more information on this). This should be less of a problem in spring and summer, but if you intend to use your barbecue all year round, I would recommend paying particular attention, after narrowing the field, to the barbecue's power output. An inadequately powered unit (see page 11 for further information) used in adverse weather conditions may give the cook needless aggravation.

Rotisserie burner

A third control knob on a wagon gas barbecue may indicate that the barbecue has a rotisserie burner or a side burner (see below). Rotisserie burners are normally positioned at the rear and base of the barbecue's grill area, directly under a narrow cage containing a quantity of rock or ceramic blocks. They are well away from the juices and fats dropping from the spitted food, but close enough to spit roast the food to crisp perfection. (The spit roasting technique is covered on pages 34–5.)

Wagon gas barbecues incorporating a rotisserie burner offer the cook a highly efficient method of spit roasting all manner of food, particularly if the height of the lid allows wide-bodied items, such as a rib of beef or a large turkey, to revolve freely with the lid down.

Rotisserie burners are generally rated at around 12,000 BTUs (3.5 kilowatts).

Side burner

The side burner is a fairly recent innovation that is proving popular with those barbecue cooks who wish to prepare sauces, soups, vegetables and hot drinks whilst using the main body of the barbecue to roast, bake and grill.

When not being used, the burner hob is normally protected by a stainless steel or aluminium cover. The cover acts as a windshield when it is raised.

Side burners are generally rated at around 8,000 BTUs (2.3 kilowatts).

Work surfaces

Apart from the most basic units, wagon gas barbecues provide a variety of work surfaces. These can be fixed, hinged or removable, and side and/or front shelves. They are usually made from cedar wood – not always of the best quality. My preference is for a close-boarded work surface because I find it annoying when items such as skewers fall through the gaps in a slatted-wood work surface.

Food grills and warming grills

The variety of grills available with the larger gas units has already been mentioned in the section on semi-portable units on page 14. The 'wagons', however, offer a greater choice. For example, some of the very large warming grills are hinged to the lid and lower casting whilst others simply rest on the sides of the lower casting. Food grills tend to be 'heavy-duty' in nature and invariably have the advantage of being split into two halves.

Heat indicators

Usually mounted to one side of the lid front, the heat indicator is well named because, although it is a thermometer, it does little more than indicate – through the words 'low', 'medium' and 'high' – what the temperature is inside the cooking housing when the lid is down. It does, however, help you to know how your barbecue performs at certain readings, thus making baking and roasting a more precise operation. (Further information on this is given on page 33.) A few units incorporate a thermometer that shows the temperature in degrees fahrenheit. These sometimes double as a meat thermometer because they can be withdrawn from the lid and used separately.

Stability

This important requirement has been covered in the 'check-point' list on page 12. However, it is worth stressing that wagon barbecues – because of their weight – need a greater degree of structural stability than the lighter-weight models. Factory assembled units tend to score on this point.

Permanent gas barbecues

The idea of installing a permanent barbecue in an outdoor leisure area (it used to be called the back garden!) appeals to many barbecue enthusiasts. The concept first became popular in California during the 1950s, most of the houses built during that period incorporated an outdoor cooking and eating area in their design.

Despite refreshingly uncertain weather, the inclusion of a permanent barbecue in garden landscapes is now fairly commonplace and may even be mentioned in estate agents' sales 'blurbs'. If the design, construction and facilities of the built-in barbecues I have seen recently are anything to go by, some agents might amplify their reference to the barbecue with the phrase 'ripe for conversion to Granny flat'!

Gas barbecues of the 'built-in' variety without 'under-carriage' are more readily available, in keeping with the increasing popularity and availability of their wheeled brethren. However, it may require some shopping around to locate what you are looking for.

Models range from single and twin burner units of around 1600 square cm (250 square inches) grill area to a giant four burner unit of approximately 4200 square cm (650 square inches). If you need extra cooking area there is a range of heavy-duty catering gas barbecues with grill areas of up to 10,800 square cm (1728 square inches). The choice extends to units with or without lids.

Without doubt the best time to tackle the design and building of a structure to accommodate your gas barbecue is when the patio/garden is being designed and built. If a new house is involved it should be possible to get matching bricks and materials so the barbecue blends in with its surroundings.

Using natural stone to build the structure has its drawbacks as it's expensive and difficult to shape. It may also appear incongruous when set against modern brick. The same may apply to the use of cheap house bricks when set against, for example, the warm honey colour of Northampton and Cotswold stone walls. For reasons of economy and ease of construction, many people opt for reconstituted stone blocks and slabs, which are available in a large range of colours and textures.

Needless to say, great care should be taken over the design and lay-out of the barbecue area because errors in design or location may not be easy to rectify at a later date.

Design basics

An essential element in the design of a permanent structure for your gas barbecue is the provision of an adequate work surface adjacent to, and level with, the barbecue's food grill. A second work surface nearby will enable another cook to work companionably alongside whilst preparing the salad, dessert, etc. The food grill(s) and work surfaces should be set at the same comfortable working height as those employed in the kitchen.

Storage cupboards are not essential, but nevertheless could prove useful for stacking away garden tools.

I reckon that a lot of barbecue parties take place in the late evening. It therefore makes sense to mount at least one good quality, adequately powerful spot-light in the cooking area (avoid positioning the light(s) behind the cook as this will create a deep shadow over the grill area). It is important that the cook can see whether his or her grilled steaks are rare, medium or well-done. Good lighting in the eating area will enable guests to appreciate the beauty of the food (and its identity!).

Installing an underground cable and fitting the lights is a job for a competent electrician – it is better to be safe and sure. On the other hand, the installation of a sink is something that can be done by most DIYers, using one of the simple push-fit plumbing systems now readily available.

If the intended location and funds permit, it might be worthwhile considering some form of canopy to provide weather protection for the cook. Incorporating a chimney in the design is useful for dispersing smoke, but this feature is more important for a charcoal-burning installation where it helps to improve up-draught.

As already mentioned, the location is very important, so do bear in mind the direction of the prevailing wind – especially if French doors are likely to be left open during cooking. Ideally the barbecue should be near the kitchen, but, if it is away from the patio or other hard-standing areas, ensure that the area next to the cooking/preparation area is paved with non-slip slabs; it is not a good idea for it to be grassed.

Even the most experienced cook will have the odd flare-up. With this in mind, site the barbecue well away from thatched buildings, trees and shrubs.

Commercial catering gas barbecues

If you happen to be associated in some way with catering, perhaps as a publican, hotelier, restaurateur, outside caterer or club catering manager, you are probably already aware of purpose-built catering gas barbecues. There are several exellent units on the market, most of which (unlike their domestic counterparts) are of British design and manufacture. In fact, in this area of the market, Britain probably leads the world. Cooking areas range from around 3715 square cm (576 square inches) to 11,146 square cm (1728 square inches).

Most models are too large and heavy for moving around, but there is one commercial unit that, despite having a large cooking area (about 7095 square cm/1100 square inches), can be handled by one moderately strong person. Its clever design allows it to be folded down in just a few seconds to a mere 19 cm (7½ inches) depth, so it can be transported by estate car. These features make this barbecue particularly suitable for the equipment hire business, Scout groups or any organisation that wants to move the barbecue about on a regular basis.

Another unit I am familiar with – which is part of a range – is one that combines cooking heat with a substantial and well-made spit roast assembly. With its heavy-duty electrically operated spit motor and removable covers, this assembly is capable of cooking a 54 kg (120 lb) pig to mouth-watering perfection in 4–5 hours.

Most commercial gas barbecues are destined for the patios and gardens of public houses, hotels, restaurants or caravan sites where they will probably be chef-operated, although a growing number of establishments encourage their patrons to try barbecuing for themselves. Each barbecue in the catering range has its own special features, but they all share the same high degree of solid construction coupled with great economy in use. Anyone organising large-scale barbecue parties – for fund raising, large families or club socials – should check with their local hire shops and suppliers of bottled gas to find out if they have commercial catering barbecues for hire. These units are capable of handling large quantities of fast-cooking foods in fairly short order, thus keeping queues moving and in good humour. Fuel costs are also low.

Tools and accessories

In keeping with the fun nature of barbecuing some of the tools and accessories border on the frivolous, but each item on display at good barbecue equipment stockists has been designed for a specific task. Newcomers to the art are advised to concentrate on a handful of tools that help make barbecuing safer and easier. Less essential tools can be added later.

Apron and gloves

For comfort and practicality, nothing beats a cloth apron, long enough to cover the knees and with one or two deep pockets in the front. Wearing a plastic-coated apron in front of a hot barbecue on a hot day is an effective way of losing weight! Buy gloves rather than mitts, and gauntlets rather than gloves, because wrists and the lower forearm need protection too! The design should allow tools to be gripped comfortably and give good protection against the radiant heat of the barbecue.

Basting brushes

Long-handled basting brushes are available but some people prefer to use a good quality 5 cm (2-inch) paint brush. It is a good idea to have two brushes – one to apply fats (oil and butter) and the other to apply sauces. The brushes' bristles should be natural – nylon or plastic are unsuitable.

Chopping board

The larger the board the better. Most kichen-bound chopping boards are too small. Ideally the board should be one of the new laminates now used by professional caterers, but a good quality hardwood board will suffice.

Cleaning brush
The problem with most grill cleaning
brushes, useful as they are, is that after just
one or two uses the fine wire bristles clog up
with fat and food debris. You then have to
clean the cleaning brush. However, the
metal scraper fixed to the brush head is
handy for scraping the upper and lower
housings when the barbecue is spring
cleaned.

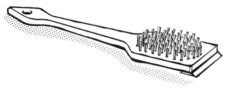

Drip pan
Roasting meat by the indirect heat method
is, I believe, a cooking technique that most

gas barbecue owners will be tempted to try.
The technique (described fully on pages
33–4) calls for a drip pan to be placed
immediately underneath the area supporting
the meat. This keeps the barbecue cleaner and
is also useful for collecting the juices from the
meat for making into gravy. A standard steel
roasting pan can be used to catch the falling
food fat and debris, but the rules of hygiene
demand that the pan be cleared and washed
soon after the food has been cooked.

Personally, I have always preferred to
use a drip pan made from aluminium foil.
The main reason is that the foil pan can be
discarded completely, thereby cutting out an
irksome cleaning task. By the way, it is much
easier to remove the pan once the contents
have partly congealed.

To make a drip pan from foil: take a 46
cm (18-inch) roll of extra-thick foil and tear
off a strip about 10 cm (4 inches) longer
than the length of the pan. Fold the foil in
half lengthways, double-fold the edges to
make 2.5 cm (1-inch) walls, flatten the foil
and lightly score a bisecting line at each
corner. Pull out and pinch the corners (as
shown opposite). Fold the corners back
tightly against the sides. The result should be
a leak-proof pan approximately 13 cm (5
inches) wide with 2.5 cm (1-inch) high walls.
To create a wider and larger pan, use wider
foil or simply fold the foil widthways.

First aid kit
The odd small burn and blister is par for the
course during a busy barbecuing year. A
spray-on burn lotion should therefore form
part of your domestic first aid kit. This
should be complemented with some plasters
and antiseptic for the odd cut for away from
home cook-outs.

Bug repellents in spray or citronella
candle form are worth having for warm
summer evenings when biting flying insects
are attracted by the party lights. If you live
in a low-lying area where insects can be a

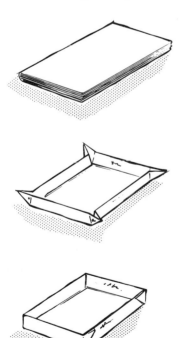

How to make a drip pan from aluminium foil

problem, you could consider investing in an electronic 'bug zapper' (like the ones in food shops). Areas up to two acres, so it is claimed, will be clear of the dreaded mosquito family if one of these somewhat expensive gadgets is installed.

Foil
Heavy-duty aluminium foil is indispensable to the barbecue cook. For making temporary drip pans (see page 19), wrapping vegetables and fruit (see page 39), protecting the protruding bits of chicken, fish, etc., and using, in the form of a crumpled ball, to remove food deposits from messy grills (see page 28).

Forks
These should be long-handled with a comfortable wooden or thermoplastic grip.

Gas lighters
Essential for owners of gas barbecues that do not incorporate a push-button igniter, but worth having as a stand-by for those who do!

Hinged wire broilers
Long-handled, chrome-plated wire broilers come in many different shapes and sizes. The square- or rectangular-shaped broiler is excellent for handling food so small it could easily fall through the grill bars – chicken wings, prawns, cocktail sausages and

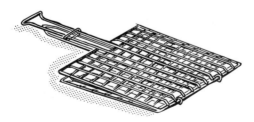

chicken livers – but make sure that the broiler bars themselves are close-spaced! The main benefit, however, is that less time is spent turning each item and, providing the broiler has been well oiled, it is less likely that food will stick to the grill.

Broilers are also available with shaped pockets which hold up to half a dozen burgers or chops. All these broilers can be used for toasting bread and rolls as well.

Particularly useful, in my view, are fish broilers (sometimes referred to as fish holders). The most popular of these is the one designed to hold a 375 g (12 oz) small whole fish, such as trout. Not so easy to find are the single fish broilers that will hold a 1 kg (2 lb) fish. They are usually heavier in quality and come with a good-sized wooden handle. Other useful versions: one that accommodates three, or four if turned head to tail, small trout (or similar) side by side; another that takes up to a dozen sardines (it looks a little like a bicycle wheel); and another that holds two flat fish side by side.

A variation on these broilers, is the flat or cylindrical-shaped wire basket designed for clamping to a spit rod. The cylindrical type allows food to tumble about freely as the spit turns.

Kitchen paper
Another great pal of the outdoor cook: sling a whole roll from the waist by a piece of string.

Knives
A good quality 'butcher' knife is a must for trimming and portioning meat. A small paring knife will be required for preparing fruit and vegetables and a good quality

carving knife is essential for serving a magnificent barbecued roast properly. Also worth having, if you have a spare one, is a bread knife. It is probable that most, if not all, of the above cutlery will come from the kitchen drawer. Do not be tempted to use the set of knives swopped for petrol coupons back in 1975 and never used: quality is important when working outside on less than perfect surfaces.

Meat thermometers

A meat thermometer helps take the guesswork out of cooking large joints and is particularly important when checking that pork is properly cooked. Meat thermometers are available in two styles: the round clock-type thermometer with a moving hand that broadly tells you if the meat you are cooking is rare, medium or well-done; the flat arrow-shaped thermometer with a column of mercury from which the temperature is read.

A false reading will occur if the tip of the probe is resting against a bone, metal spit rod or (more difficult to discern) in a pocket of fat.

A quick-registering meat thermometer is an important accessory when spit roasting a whole pig.

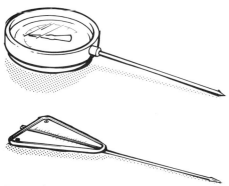

Pots and pans

Cooking pans must have long handles for safety and comfort in use. They should also have thick bases. If the pot or pan handles are wooden or plastic, protect them from the heat with a thick wrapping of heavy-duty aluminium foil.

Skewers

Of the large variety of metal skewers commonly available, those with flat or twisted blades are best for chunky pieces of meat and vegetables. Small-diameter, round-bladed skewers tend to leave the food behind when turned. A skewer that is 50 cm (20 inches) or longer can accommodate and evenly cook about twice the normal amount of food if it is laid along the length of the food grill rather than across it.

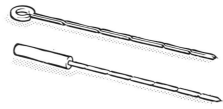

It is possible to find flat-bladed skewers with attractive cast metal heads as handles but, like other all-metal skewers, these need handling with gloves.

Most of the medium to long skewers have wooden, formed plastic or PVC covered handles.

A skewer that is worth looking out for is the twin-bladed skewer reminiscent of a kirby-grip or hair pin.

Bamboo skewers – normally 20–30 cm (8–12 inches) long – are traditionally used for satay and other small appetisers, but soak them in water before using to prevent burning.

Spatulas

These should be long-handled with a broad blade for turning such items as burgers.

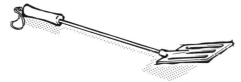

Twin-bladed spatulas (scissor action) are available; these handle flat foods in a tong-like manner.

Spit and spit motor (rotisserie)
Relatively few gas barbecues are supplied with a spit roast assembly, that is, a spit rod, motor and support brackets. However, the bottom casting on most units (other than the small portable barbecues) is pre-drilled to accept the equipment. As a general rule, most manufacturers include a rotisserie in their list of accessories.

Most spit motors are battery operated (the best utilise two HP2 batteries), but one or two more expensive models have powerful electrically operated spit motors. The plastic housing of the very cheap single-battery operated motor is liable to melt when it is next to the barbecue's hot lower housing. Wrapping two or three layers of heavy-duty aluminium foil round the motor gives it some protection.

The spit rod should be able to support at least one fat chicken without deflecting unduly, and the thumbscrews securing the meat tines to the rod should be sturdy enough to be tightened firmly without stripping the threads.

Tongs
For my money, tongs are the single most important tool in the cook's arsenal and worth shopping around for. Look for a pair that suits the size and strength of your hand. Like all other barbecue food-handling tools the tongs should be long-handled and the grips made of wood or thermoplastic. The mouth and teeth of the tongs should be

gentle – sharp-pointed teeth may pierce the sealed surface of the food and allow precious juices to escape. A good pre-purchase test of the tongs' ability to handle small pieces of food is to grasp and pick up a pencil. Two basic types are available – scissor tongs and sprung metal tongs. Be wary of cheap scissor tongs, they have a tendency to 'cross their legs' and send the sausage, or whatever you are attempting to manipulate, over your shoulder!

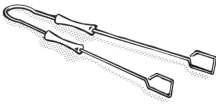

Wok
A wok makes the perfect partner for a gas barbecue, so if you like stir-fried food, it is worth adding it to your battery of barbecue equipment. If, happily, you already use a wok in the kitchen, why not buy another (they can be bought for remarkably little from Chinese stores and the like) and reserve it for vegetable stir-fries for your non-meat eating friends. (Further information on woks is given on pages 36–8.)

Safety first

Your first task before assembling your new barbecue – or commencing to use a factory pre-assembled unit – is to spend time reading and digesting the notes on safety prominently featured in the manufacturer's assembly and operating manual. It should be a case of safety first and 'christening' your barbecue second!

Retain the manual in case you require spare parts or need to check the safety points. For the record, here are some basic 'dos' and 'don'ts'.

○ *Do* ensure that the outlet pressure marked on the gas regulator is the same as the pressure required by the barbecue (details are given on the barbecue's data badge). If in doubt, check with your local gas retailer.

It is essential that a low pressure regulator with an outlet pressure of 28 mbar (to B.S. 3016) is used.

○ *Do* carry out a leak test before fitting the hose, valve and regulator (all normally supplied interconnected, although with some models you will have to supply and fit the regulator) to the barbecue control panel. To do this:

1. Make up a soap and water solution.
2. Take your full butane gas cylinder and the hose, valve and regulator assembly (or a pre-assembled unit) to an outside area and connect the regulator to the cylinder valve.
3. Turn the control knob(s) of the barbecue valve(s) to the off position.
4. Turn the gas supply fully on at the cylinder.

2
GETTING TO KNOW YOUR BARBECUE
—

Screw-on type regulator

Quick-coupling type regulator

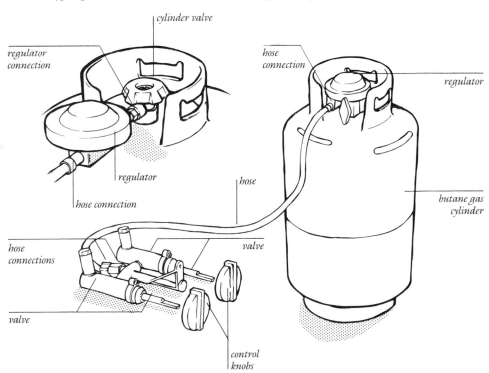

Parts to test for leaks (designs may vary)

5. Apply soapy mixture to all the connection points from, and including, the cylinder valve to the valve(s) at the end of the hose (see page 23).

6. Check each connection point for bubbles caused by leaks. Tighten any leaking connections (any item that persistently leaks must be replaced).

7. Turn off the gas supply at the cylinder and turn the control knob(s) to the 'high' position to release the pressure in the hose. Disconnect the regulator from the cylinder and fit the assembly to the barbecue following the manufacturer's instructions.

○ *Do* fully close the cylinder valve when the barbecue is not being used.

○ *Do* store the barbecue disconnected from the cylinder.

○ *Do* store the cylinder outdoors in a well-ventilated space.

○ *Do* keep the cylinder vertical at all times.

○ *Do* keep the lid of the barbecue open before lighting the gas burner(s).

○ *Do* keep the area immediately around the barbecue clear of any other flammable liquids and vapours and allow at least 75 cm (30 inches) space between the barbecue and any wood.

○ *Do* keep children and pets away from the barbecue when hot.

○ *Don't* store or use petrol, or other flammable vapours and liquids near the barbecue.

○ *Don't* store the cylinder of butane gas in direct sunlight.

○ *Don't* smoke or use an open flame when testing for gas leaks!

○ *Don't* adjust or alter the regulator.

○ *Don't* use your gas barbecue indoors or in any confined, unventilated area. If using the shelter of a garage, site the barbecue near the *open* door of the garage.

Heat distribution

Most gas barbecues, with one or two exceptions, have roughly the same burner configuration. This is certainly true of the small portable units. They have a single rectangular-shaped burner (usually referred to as a ribbon burner) running along the centre of the lower casting. The much larger wagon and pedestal barbecues, whether single or twin burner units, usually have an H-shaped burner. In some models the open ends of the burner are closed and the burner is a squared figure of eight shape. The shape and size of the burner and its power output, in relation to the cooking area, influences the manner and speed in which the food on the grill is cooked.

Experience will eventually tell you where the 'hot' and 'cool' spots are, but a simple way to find the heat distribution pattern (its fingerprints) is to do, what I call, 'the toast test'.

You need a sliced white loaf. Choose a calm day for the test, light the burner(s) in the usual manner, close the lid and leave the unit to warm up for about 10 minutes. Then turn the control knob(s) to the medium setting and leave the barbecue for a further 3–4 minutes. Open the lid, cover the surface of the food grill(s) with slices of bread, cutting them to fit if necessary, and leave for about 2 minutes (see below). Turn the gas off. Using tongs, remove the slices of bread from the grill, turning and placing them on

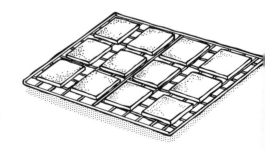

The toast test

a suitable flat surface. Take care to place the toasted bread toasted-side up in exactly the same order as they were on the barbecue. The pattern revealed by the gradation of colour should clearly indicate where the hottest and coolest spots on the grill are.

Conduct the test just before tea-time, toast the other side and everyone can enjoy the result of your labours!

Problems and solutions

Burner(s) will not light

possible cause	The cylinder of gas is almost empty.
solution	*Replace with a full cylinder.*
possible cause	The cylinder valve is not fully open.
solution	*Fully open the cylinder valve (turn the valve anti-clockwise).*

possible cause	The valve outlets are not properly seated in the venturi.
solution	*Fully locate the valve in the venturi (when properly in position, the gas jets are visible through the 'window' in the venturi).*
possible cause	One or more of the gas jets or venturis is clogged (perhaps with spider webs or cocoons – quite possible if the barbecue hasn't been used for some time).
solution	*Clean the inside of the venturi tubes with a bottle brush. Carefully clean the jet orifices with fine wire or the tip of a round toothpick – do not enlarge the hole.*

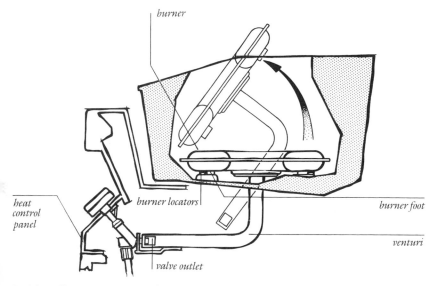

Position of burner, venturi and valve (designs may vary)

burner
heat control panel
burner locators
valve outlet
burner foot
venturi

possible cause | The venturis are not properly seated.

solution | *Check that the retaining spring, if used, is properly engaged.*

possible cause | A sharp kink in the flexible gas hose.

solution | *Re-position the cylinder to straighten the hose.*

possible cause | The igniter is not working.

solution | *(a) Check the assembly instructions to ascertain if the gap between the electrode and electrode cover is correct (if it is correct, a spark should be visible);*
(b) ensure that all wires are intact and connected;
(c) check the ceramic component for cracks.
(If a new igniter assembly is required, use a long match to light the burner in the meantime.)

possible cause | A defective valve or regulator.

solution | *If you suspect either of the above items are faulty, remove the hose from the barbecue and take it, along with the regulator and cylinder, to an authorised servicing bottle gas dealer for inspection.*

Burners provide insufficient heat

possible cause | The barbecue is not given sufficient time to warm up.

solution | *Increase the warm-up time by several minutes to allow for low air temperatures and strong breezes.*

possible cause | The venturis and gas jets are not properly aligned.

solution | *Fully locate the valve in the venturi.*

possible cause | Some of the vents in the burner assembly are clogged with food debris.

solution | *Brush clean (using a brass or stainless steel bristle brush).*

possible cause | An excessive amount of volcanic rock is used.

solution | *Remove sufficient rock to allow a close-packed single layer only.*

possible cause | One, or more, of the gas jets or venturis is clogged.

solution | *Clean the inside of the venturi tubes with a bottle brush. Carefully clean the jet orifices with fine wire or the tip of a round toothpick.*

possible cause | The volcanic rock is heavily permeated with food debris and fats.

solution | *(a) Wash the rocks in hot water to which a mild detergent has been added. Change the water and repeat as necessary. Make sure the volcanic rock is thoroughly dry before using for cooking. Dry it either in the barbecue with the lid down or in the kitchen oven;*

(b) alternatively, burn the rocks clean – see Care and Cleaning on page 28.

Flashback (flame in or around the venturi)
If flashback should occur, immediately shut off the barbecue burner controls and then turn the cylinder valve off.

possible cause · The venturis have become blocked when the barbecue has cooled.
solution · *Clean the inside of the tube with a bottle brush.*

possible cause · The venturis are not properly seated.
solution · *Check that the retaining spring (if used) is present and engaged.*

possible cause · The valve outlets are not properly seated in the venturi.
solution · *Fully locate the valve in the venturi.*

possible cause · The vents in the burner assembly are clogged.
solution · *Brush clean, using a brass or stainless steel bristle brush. (If a wire brush is unavailable, clear the blocked vents with a piece of fine wire or a round toothpick.)*

possible cause · The barbecue is exposed to strong winds.
solution · *Shield the middle/lower half of the barbecue from the wind (or turn off the gas and move the barbecue to a more sheltered position).*

Burner flame is excessively yellow (see below)

possible cause · The burner holes are clogged.
solution · *Brush clean with a brass or stainless steel bristle brush.*

possible cause · The venturi tubes are blocked.
solution · *Clean the inside of the venturi tubes with a bottle brush.*

possible cause · The venturis are not properly located on the valve outlets.
solution · *Check that the retaining spring, if used, is properly engaged.*

correct colour

incorrect colour

Correct and incorrect burner flame colour

Care and cleaning

One of the major benefits of a gas barbecue is the certainty that it will be ready when you want it with ease and speed. It follows that most gas barbecues will be used regularly – what better way is there to revive a tired mind and body than the thought that in a short time a juicy steak or two will be sizzling away on the barbecue grill. There is a small drawback (or a definite 'plus' if you are calorie counting) common to all barbecues: the volume of fat that direct grilling produces. Most of the fat falls on to the volcanic rock (the wide, concave grill bars on some units reduce that amount by roughly fifty per cent) and some gets through the rock layer into the lower housing. Apart from hygienic considerations, allowing the barbecue to get progressively gungy is counter-productive: volcanic rock heavily impregnated with fat and food debris can significantly reduce the radiant (cooking) heat from the rock. Therefore it makes sense to clean the barbecue regularly.

Basic clean

Cleaning your barbecue after every cook-out is certainly worth doing, not only for the reasons already mentioned but because your barbecue will be ready for instant action the next time you want to use it.

Two elements in particular require regular attention – the volcanic rock and the cooking grill(s). Cleaning the rock can be undertaken in two ways:
(a) remove the cooked food from the grill(s) and, with the barbecue still alight, close the lid and turn the burner control knob(s) to the high setting. Leave the barbecue for 5–10 minutes – long enough for most, if not all, of the fats and food residues to burn off. During the first few minutes of 'burn-off' a considerable amount of smoke will probably come out from under the lid, so if you follow this method at the end of the cook-out make sure the eating area is up wind of the barbecue! Otherwise, light the barbecue and follow this method at any time before the next cook-out;
(b) just before a cook-out, remove the food grill(s) and turn over the grease-laden rocks by hand. Add a few extra minutes to the warm-up period to burn off the fats. A classic case of killing two birds with one stone.

Cleaning the food grill(s) does require time and effort, but cleaning the grill each time to a state of pristine perfection is, in my opinion, an unnecessary and off-putting chore. Some people swear by wet newspaper: spread several sheets of newspaper on the ground, soak them well and lay the grill(s) on top. Place several more sheets on top of the grill(s) and soak it all well. When you remove the grills the encrusted fat and food debris should be left behind with the newsprint.

A simple way to clean the grill is to leave it in position while burning the fat from the rocks. Any charred food particles can be removed with a wire brush.

However, using a brush with fine wire bristles on a grill from which food has only just been removed means the bristles get clogged with grease. My preference is to use aluminium foil: loosely crumple a good-size piece and, with a gloved hand, firmly press the foil down on to the bars of the grill, scrubbing it up and down (the foil forms snugly over the bars) to remove all the encrustations. A wipe over with some kitchen paper and the barbecue is ready for the next cook-out. During the warm up period for the next barbecue, the heat will 'cauterise' the bars, though it's a good idea to wipe them over with some kitchen paper before placing the food on the grill.

If you have a large sink then occasionally give the grill(s) a good scrub in hot water with a mild soap or detergent.

Annual spring-clean

Giving your gas barbecue a thorough clean up once a year (twice, if you are an 'all-year rounder') will help to keep the unit in tip-top working order. Proceed as follows:

1. Remove the food grill(s), volcanic rock, grate and burner assembly. (The electrode assembly – if the unit has an igniter – can also be removed if desired.)

2. Cover the valve outlets with aluminium foil.

3. Scrape and wire brush the inside surfaces of the upper and lower housings to remove food debris. Clean off the surface with hot water and mild detergent using a scrubbing brush or scouring pad.

Note: if you want to use an oven cleaner, make sure it is safe to use on aluminium.

4. Brush the surface of the burner(s) with a wire brush. Clean out any clogged vents with a piece of stiff wire.

5. Clean the food grill(s) by giving them a good soak and scrub in hot water with a mild soap or detergent. Do the same with the warming grill, if the barbecue has one.

6. Wash off grease marks or white spots (caused by oxidation) from the exterior of the upper housing – again using hot water with a mild soap or detergent.

Note: if the exterior surfaces of your barbecue look rather bleached and grubby, it might be worth buying, from your local hardware store or barbecue stockist, a spray-can of heat-resistant paint.

7. Remove the foil from the valve outlets and replace the burner (ensuring the valve outlets are inside the venturi). Replace the grate, volcanic rock and the food grill(s).

8. If the barbecue has a window in its lid, clean the glass when it is cold. Use hot water and a mild cleanser. *Do not* use a commercial oven cleaner.

9. Clean out the drip can.

10. Clean and treat the wood shelving with an appropriate wood preservative or stain.

11. Tighten up all nuts and bolts in the frame assembly.

3

COOKING TECHNIQUES
—

My dictionary informs me that 'technique' is everything concerned with the mechanical part of an artistic performance. However, as far as I'm concerned all successful 'performances' by barbecue cooks are founded on good technique and become outstanding when topped with a dash of flair and a sprinkling of theatre. In my book the main objective of the artist/barbecue cook is to produce food so mouth-watering in appearance and so redolent of nose-twitching aromas that his or her audience will devour anything put in front of it and hasten back for more. It is a good idea to allow for '*al fresco* appetite' by doubling up normal 'in house' quantities.

Grilling

It used to be said in the army that even a Drill Sergeant's discarded army boot tasted good if it was grilled. And of all the various barbecue cooking techniques, grilling is the most popular, straightforward and widely practiced. In many people's eyes 'grilling' is synonymous with 'barbecuing', not surprising perhaps when both the words and cooking technique have been closely related for several centuries.

The technique involves cooking food directly over radiant heat. Different foods require different levels of heat to produce optimum succulence, colour and flavour when fully cooked. A gas barbecue does this particularly well because the cooking temperature can be adjusted up or down in the same way as one would control the heat of a gas hob or cooker.

Grilling requires constant attention, so anything that can be cooked in 30–40 minutes or less is suitable: chicken and turkey portions, chops, steaks, sausages, hamburgers, kebabs, whole fish and fish steaks are good examples. One exception might be something like butterflied leg of new season lamb, where the grilling time might be closer to 50 minutes.

Bear in mind that the heat from below hits only one surface of the food, therefore foods with two main surfaces – steaks (meat or fish) – lead the field, but hamburgers, chops and whole fish do just as well.

General guidelines on grilling times are given in the chart on page 141, but do remember that air temperature and wind strength can have a marked effect on cooking times. For example, having used a medium heat setting to grill a steak – for, say, 8 minutes each side – one Saturday lunchtime, you might find the following Saturday, when the weather is cooler and windier, that the same size steak requires the highest heat setting for, say, 10 minutes per side. In these circumstances, especially if it is raining, it would be prudent to keep the barbecue lid closed. In fact, grilling in this fashion produces, in my opinion, a more flavoursome steak. After all, it is the smoke, created by the steak juices falling on to the hot lava rock, that gives the food its distinctive colour, aroma and flavour; so holding the smoke captive benefits your steak rather than letting it titillate the noses of your neighbours.

Grilling (direct heat cooking) procedure
1. Remove the food grill(s) before igniting the gas and brush the grill(s) with some groundnut (peanut) oil or similar. Alternatively, rub a little fat cut from the meat over the grill surface. (If cooking the food in a dish or in foil over direct heat, don't bother greasing the grill(s).)
2. Ignite the gas burners at the high heat setting (with the lid open) and then close the lid. Allow the lava rock to get hot enough to radiate adequate grilling heat – this could take 3–10 minutes depending upon the barbecue model and the weather.
3. Replace the food grill(s) just before cooking the food.

4. Turn the gas control knob(s) to the required setting (more on this below).
5. Position the food on the grill(s) (avoid crowding the grill surface – especially with fat-laden food such as chicken portions, hamburgers and sausages).

Grilling hints

○ Brush a little oil or melted butter over one surface of the meat (steaks, chops, kebabs, cutlets or escalopes) or fish (whole or steaks). If desired, pre-season the oil with herbs (fresh or dried), barbecue spices, soy sauce or Worcestershire sauce (using one or a combination of flavours), or season to taste after the oil has been applied.

○ If a thick basting sauce is used – one containing sugar, jam, ketchup or honey – brush it on during the final few minutes of cooking. If applied too early, especially if using a moderately high temperature setting, the meat may finish up with an unpleasantly charred surface.

○ Grill one side of the meat for the time recommended in the recipe or cooking time chart (page 141). Brush the uncooked surface with oil or butter (seasoned to taste), turn the food over and complete the cooking cycle.

○ Marinate meat for a few hours or overnight in the refrigerator to tenderise and add flavour to the meat. A less expensive lean cut, like chuck, will benefit from an oil-based marinade.

○ Provide two or three flavoured butters (page 133) for your guests to allow them to choose their preferred flavour.

○ Use long-handled, square-headed tongs with 'soft jaws' to turn steaks (see above). Avoid tongs that have sharp teeth that may pierce the meat and cause loss of precious juices. (If you have to use a fork, try to pierce the fat so the meat surface remains intact.)

○ Fish-shaped hinged wire broilers, although inexpensive, are worth their

Turning a steak with square-headed tongs

Salmon steaks in a square, hinged wire broiler

weight in gold for anyone intending to regularly grill whole fish. Rectangular or square hinged wire broilers also make life a lot easier when grilling fish steaks (see above), flat meats or a quantity of small items such as chicken wings. (More information concerning broilers is on page 20.)

○ Thaw frozen meat whilst it marinates. Simply keep the meat in the marinade, turning it a few times if it is not immersed, until it is defrosted.

○ As a general rule, use a low to medium heat setting on your gas barbecue when dealing with fish, vegetables and fruit, and the medium heat setting when dealing with beef, poultry, pork and lamb. (The high heat setting is normally used for searing the meat and for preheating and cleaning the barbecue.)

How to test if fish is cooked

○ Test if fish is cooked by prodding it gently with a fork: the fish is done when the flesh divides naturally (see above).
○ Flare-up (a sudden blaze) is unfortunately the bane of far too many barbecue cooks. However, it should be something the gas barbecue chef rarely has to contend with as the prime cause is excessive heat, and heat is the one thing he or she has complete control of. A secondary cause is grilling excessively fatty food, and this can be compounded ten times over by crowding the grill with the fatty food. The result of doing this, unless you move fast, could be the food's cremation and some hungry guests.

If you do create a flare-up – perhaps by leaving the control knob(s) at high after the warm-up period is over – quickly slide the food away from the flame. Normally it is only a matter of seconds before the flame burns itself out.

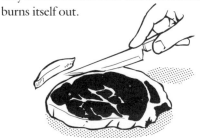

Trimming a steak of excess fat

Chicken portions tend to suffer most because the skin is quickly coated in a black, sooty film. If this happens, rescue the blackened piece and wipe clean with kitchen paper before returning it to the grill.

Grilling kebabs

Impaling food on a sharpened stick and grilling it over the dying embers of a fire probably gave our cave man ancestors the same pleasure as his twentieth century, gas barbecuing counterpart using a fancy metal skewer.

Meat, poultry, fish, vegetables, fruit and bread can all be cooked on a skewer and give the chef free rein to produce an infinite variety of food which pleases both the eye and the palate. Kebab permutations can produce exciting taste sensations where the juices from meat and fruit intermingle and blend. Marinating the food beforehand gives the cook even greater scope.

The basic procedure for skewer cooking is covered in the notes on grilling (pages 30–1), but here are a few extra tips.
○ Oil metal skewers before threading on the ingredients. Bamboo skewers, traditionally used for satay, should be soaked in water before use to help stop them burning.
○ When skewering chunks of fish, leave the skin intact as this will help to hold the flesh together whilst cooking.
○ Do not crowd food on a skewer. Leave small gaps between chunks of meat so the heat can circulate. Small pieces of fruit, and vegetables such as green pepper, can be used as spacers to hold the meat apart.
○ To assist even cooking, either make up kebabs with foods that have similar cooking times or part-cook the slower-cooking foods to even out grilling times.
○ For mixed vegetable kebabs, parboil the slower cooking items, like corn on the cob pieces, carrots and small onions, to help

even up the cooking times.

○ If your gas barbecue has a warming grill, use it to support and gently cook vegetable kebabs whilst grilling meat-only kebabs on the food grill below. The vegetable kebabs can be finished off directly on the food grill, if wished.

○ Skewers with wooden handles are easy to hold and turn. Use oven gloves or a barbecue gauntlet to turn stainless steel skewers. Highly practical, but difficult to locate, are two-pronged skewers. Flat- or square-bladed skewers hold and turn the kebabs better than round-sectioned skewers. (More about skewers in the section on Tools and Accessories.)

○ Trim excess fat from meat to help prevent flare-ups.

Roasting and baking

In most users' eyes, certainly in mine, the ease and convenience of using a gas barbecue is the biggest benefit to the cook. A close second is the extraordinarily wide range of cooking techniques that can be employed, especially with a twin burner system. The cooking technique that stands out is indirect heat cooking. Using a twin burner gas barbecue for this is like using your kitchen oven for roasting and baking foods. Baking in the barbecue, given only a little practice and experience, is highly satisfactory, and roasting joints this way gives mouth-watering results. Several of the recipes in this book use this technique. May I suggest that you also use the technique for cooking some of your favourite recipes. As well as roasting (whole birds, large joints and thick pieces of meat) and baking (pies, bread, cakes, puddings and pizzas), you can include a nourishing casserole in your repertoire too.

For the best results when baking, the barbecue should have a thermometer incorporated in its lid. The thermometers on the more expensive models normally show the temperature in degrees fahrenheit coupled, perhaps, with the words 'low', 'medium' and 'high'. The less expensive models normally give just the words as a guide to the air temperature under the closed lid. Experience will help you decide which heat setting works best; the following table is only a general guide, because the power and capacity of the range of models varies considerably.

Low setting: 120–130°C/200–250°F
Medium setting: 170–220°C/325–425°F
High setting: 260–340°C/500–650°F

If your twin burner gas barbecue does not have a thermometer in its lid you can still bake the odd pie. Set the control knob to medium (or perhaps slightly higher if your unit is rated at 27,000 BTUs/7.8 kilowatts or less, or the air temperature is cool) and check the pie, or whatever, after about the same cooking time as you would if using your kitchen oven. It's worth having a go. So next time you roast the weekend joint in your gas barbecue, have a freshly made fruit pie ready. When the joint is cooked and removed, pop in the pie and, by the time the meat has been rested, carved and consumed, the pie should be beautifully baked. A wonderful way to use your barbecue to the full.

When roasting, follow the cooking times and internal temperatures given in the recipes or in the cooking time chart on page 140.

Indirect heat cooking procedure

1. Position a drip pan/tin or one made from aluminium foil (see Tools and Accessories) under the food grill to one side of the barbecue. The drip pan should be large enough to catch fats and juices falling from the food being cooked, but not so large that

it intrudes into the other half of the unit.
(Omit the drip pan if you intend baking.)
2. With the lid open, ignite the gas burner
(at the high setting) on the opposite side to
the drip pan.
3. Close the lid and leave for 5–10 minutes.
4. Position the food on the grill over the
unlit burner (see below) and re-close the lid.
5. Adjust the temperature as required. (If
placing the food on the barbecue
immediately after ignition, remember to
adjust the heat setting after the warm-up
time!)

Note: some barbecue models have very
limited space between the grill bars and the
rock layer for even a very shallow drip pan.
If this is the situation, remove sufficient rock
from the grate on the *unlit* side *before*
igniting the opposite gas burner. Do not
place the removed rock on the lit side as it
will reduce the cooking temperature and
extend the cooking time. If you do follow
this procedure, use a steel drip pan rather
than one made from foil.

*Roasting meat on the barbecue with indirect
heat, using a drip pan*

Spit roasting

Spit roasting is regarded by some people as
the only true method of roasting. In their
eyes oven roasting is a form of baking
because the food is cooked by indirect heat.
Be that as it may, watching a handsome cut
of meat – rib of beef, loin of pork, saddle or
leg of lamb, a plump chicken or two, a duck,
turkey or pheasant – slowly revolving on a
spit can be a riveting, almost mesmerising,
experience, and it makes the perfect prelude
to the meal itself. Appetites tend to increase
with the developing beauty of the roast!

Other than the small fully portable
units, most gas barbecues can incorporate a
spit roast assembly (rotisserie). Relatively
few gas barbecues have the equipment as a
standard feature but the sets are usually
available from good stockists. (Further
details about spits and spit motors are in the
section on Tools and Accessories.)

Spit roasting is normally carried out on
an open barbecue, but this method wastes
energy because the heat warms the air above
the barbecue. The most efficient method
(although not one for the avid spit-watcher)
is for the food to be spit-roasted with the lid
closed throughout. The captive heat
shortens the cooking time and allows the
spit roasting to be carried out in inclement
weather. With this in mind, some of the
larger gas barbecues have deep lids that are
capable, when closed, of accommodating a 9
kg (20 lb) turkey.

Another aid to spit roasting deeper
chested birds and thicker joints is a
split food grill. Removing one of the grill
halves provides more space whilst the
grill remaining *in situ* can be used briefly,
during spit roasting, to rustle up some
appetisers.

Follow the cooking times and internal
temperatures given in the recipes, or in the
cooking time chart on page 142.

Spit roasting procedure
In order for the roast to rotate smoothly and
cook evenly, it must be properly balanced on
the spit rod. Poorly balanced meat will
rotate in fits and starts, be unevenly cooked

and increase wear on the spit motor. With practice, you should be able to pass the spit rod through the centre of the food mass regardless of its shape.

1. Make sure there is a set of tines (prongs) on the rod with its prongs pointing away from the handle.

2. If spit roasting a leg of lamb or pork, insert the spit to run alongside the leg or shank bones. If spit roasting a rib roast, or shoulder or loin of pork, beef or lamb, insert the spit near the bones at one corner of the roast and push diagonally through the meat until it emerges close to the opposite corner. If spit roasting poultry, push the tip of the spit through the 'parson's nose' (tail vent) into the body cavity and out through the flap of skin at the neck.

3. Push the prongs deep into the meat, slide the other set of tines down the rod and push them deep into the meat; then secure the thumbscrews. If necessary, use string to tie poultry and game birds into a compact shape. (Essential where there is a restricted amount of space between the spit and grill or bed of rocks.)

4. Check that the spit is evenly balanced: rotate the laden spit slowly on your palms (see below), if there is no tendency to roll suddenly from any position the balance is good. If it does roll unevenly, re-skewer the food to correct the imbalance.

5. Remove the food grill(s) and place a drip pan directly on the rocks, parallel to, and

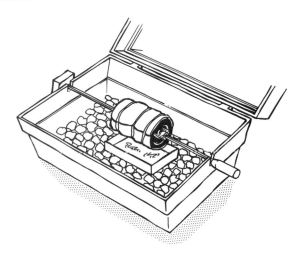

Spit roasting meat on the barbecue using a drip pan

slightly in front of, where the food-laden spit will be. Use a pan, which must be made of steel, that is narrow in width and fairly shallow in depth – especially if there is comparatively little space between the top of the rock and the underside of the grill bars. Fill it three-quarters full with water.

6. With the lid open, ignite the gas burners at the high heat setting. Close the lid and leave for 5–10 minutes.

7. Position the food-laden spit and adjust the spit motor so that the meat on the spit turns up and away from the cook, allowing the juices to fall into the drip pan (see above). Close the lid or leave it open if wished and adjust the temperature as required (more on this following).

Spit roasting hints

○ Avoid using an excessively high heat as this will make the liquid in the drip pan evaporate quickly. If it does disappear quickly, carefully pour in some more liquid. *But never pour water into a drip pan that has a high concentration of hot fat.*

○ Use leftover beer or wine to fill the drip pan if you intend using the fat-enriched liquid (perhaps with added herbs) as a savoury baste.

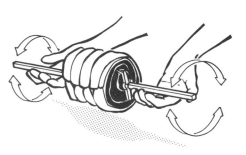

The spit balance test

○ Unless marinated, brush the impaled food with oil. Once should be sufficient.

Smoke-cooking

One advantage a gas barbecue has over its kitchen-bound counterpart is that the open air appliance can be used to smoke-cook meat and fish. The two primary aims of this highly satisfying technique are to impart a stronger colour and a richer flavour to the food. When roasted by the indirect heat cooking method (page 33), a chicken or turkey will take on a singularly attractive appearance. However, when enveloped for 20–30 minutes in scented smoke, a dramatic change occurs in the appearance and colour of the food and the flavour becomes that little bit more piquant. Apart from poultry, ham, pork, venison, spare ribs, sausages, lamb, kidneys and a variety of fish – such as salmon, trout, mackerel, eel and oysters – are excellent fare for smoke-cooking. (It is not unknown to smoke cheese in a gas barbecue, though the heat control has to be at its lowest setting and a close eye kept on the cheese.)

A growing number of barbecue stockists carry the two major aromatic smoking woods currently available – hickory and mesquite (available in both chunks or chips) – plus the packeted wood and herb smoking mixtures. Wood that is going to be used for smoke-cooking should be kept in a bucket of water so that it is well soaked before it is dropped on to the hot rocks. The wood and herb mixtures should also be well soaked before use. Indigenous hardwoods suitable for 'hot smoking' include beech, oak, cherry, apple, alder, sycamore, poplar and vine. If desired, the natural fragrance of the wood can be enhanced by adding sprigs of rosemary or thyme to the fire-bed. Do not use pine or other resinous woods, these have an unpleasant effect on the food.

Experience will help you to judge how much wood and when it should be added for the best result. I find that adding a small chunk of hickory (roughly the size of a duck egg) to the hot rock about half way through roasting a 1.5 kg (3½ lb) chicken, or some 30 minutes before a turkey is cooked, turns the skin of the bird an attractive golden mahogany colour and gives the flesh a delicate smoked flavour that suits my taste. For those who prefer a stronger taste, make the smoke earlier in the cooking time.

Even if you produce the smoke immediately when smoke-cooking small fish, it will have a limited effect.

If you like baked beans, try placing them in an open pot alongside the meat you are smoke-cooking, stir them occasionally and they will take on a pleasant smoky flavour.

To give smoke-cooked roast meat an even more dramatic appearance, brush it with a suitable glaze (included in the appropriate recipes) about 15 minutes before the end of cooking. Applying the glaze too soon may caramelise the surface of the meat to an excessive degree.

To extend the fairly brief period of a handful of wood chips, wrap the water-soaked chips tightly in heavy-duty aluminium foil, make small holes all over it and place it on the grill or directly on to the hot rocks.

Wok-cooking

For the past 5,000 years or so the wok has been the cornerstone of the Chinese kitchen. This round-bottomed 'frying-pan' (wok is the Cantonese word for pan) has become familiar throughout the western hemisphere, because of its stir-frying role in countless Chinese restaurants. But its versatility as a cooking implement equally adept at deep and shallow frying, braising and 'steaming' is perhaps not so well known. Judging from audience reaction to my stir-frying exploits at many barbecue demonstrations, its natural affinity to the barbecue is not well known either. Anyway, I'm happy to add 'wok-ing' to the other cooking techniques in this book.

Once you have purchased a wok and tried out the few recipes included in Part Four, I hope you will feel encouraged to experiment further via the many excellent books that are available on Chinese cooking. Incidentally, the wok does a great job roasting chestnuts on the barbecue!

A gas barbecue, with its infinitely variable heat control system, lends itself to handling the demands of wok cooking: from a high heat for stir-frying, to a low heat for braising. However, before rushing out to buy a wok it's a good idea to check that your barbecue is suitable for the task. As a rule, the larger the barbecue and the greater its BTU or kilowatt rating the better. However, even if your barbecue is one of the smaller patio units, rated at between 20,000 and 25,000 BTUs (5.8 and 7.3 kilowatts), this level of heat should be sufficient to bring the oil in the wok to the required stir-fry temperature, providing the width of the cooking area is enough to allow the base of the wok to rest completely on the grate. Removing the layer of lava rock from beneath where the wok will be sitting will increase the heat striking the wok.

Individual woks, about 36 cm (14 inches) in diameter at the rim, can generally be purchased, for remarkably little money, from hardware and departmental stores, catering equipment suppliers and Chinese stores. A good quality Chinese wok constructed from carbon steel will feel quite heavy when picked up by the handle, despite its thin wall. For ease of use, especially when stir-frying, buy a wok with a single long wooden handle. One with a slightly flattened base is ideal if you will be using it

in the kitchen on either a gas or electric hob as well. Try to buy a wok complete with a dome-shaped lid; failing that, buy one separately or, as a temporary measure, use the lid from a frying pan.

Although kitchen tools could, at a pinch, be used, it is better to purchase a purpose-made, long-handled wok stirrer/ scoop. Other items, such as the cleaning brush (made from stiff bamboo slivers and looking like a shaving brush), are not essential but may be of help.

Breaking in and caring for your wok

When breaking in a new wok it is necessary to remove the protective coating of machine oil. Do this by washing and scrubbing the surface with strong detergent. Wash off the detergent, thoroughly dry the wok and liberally smear the surface with cooking oil. Set the wok on the rocks or fire-grate with the heat set at high. Leave it until the oil reaches smoking point, remove it from the heat and pour in about half a cup of cooking oil, turning the wok carefully several times to ensure the oil coats the whole surface. Once again heat the wok until the oil reaches smoking point. Discard the oil and wipe the surface well with kitchen paper. The wok is now ready for use.

During cooking protect the base of the wooden handle from burning. To do this, wrap the first 10 cm (4 inches) or so with two or three layers of heavy-duty aluminium foil.

At the end of each cooking session, add some hot water to the wok whilst it is still over the heat. Clean the surface with a mildly abrasive scouring pad (or a bamboo brush) to remove the food debris. Pour away the soiled water and wipe the wok with a cloth. Finish drying the wok over the burner heat. Before storing your wok in a dry place, smear the inside liberally with cooking oil.

After several uses your wok will take on

a dark patina, inside and out, that will eventually darken to black. This darkening is to be cherished as it will add a subtle enrichment to your stir-fried dishes. Do not be tempted to burnish the metal back to its original pristine condition.

Wok-cooking procedure
1. Remove the food grill. Remove the layer of lava rock from beneath where the wok will be sitting, if wished.
2. Ignite the gas burners at the high heat setting (with the lid open) and then close the lid. Leave for 5–10 minutes.
3. Turn the gas control knob(s) to the required setting (more on this below).
4. Position the wok in the fire-grate and add the stir-frying ingredients as required.

Stir-frying hints
○ Ensure your prepared ingredients are as dry as possible before placing them in the hot oil. Excess moisture will cause the hot oil to spit up from the wok.
○ Remember to turn the wok so that the cooking surface is coated with oil; dry patches could make the food stick or burn.
○ Unless indicated otherwise in the recipe, use high heat and lift and turn the contents from the bottom of the wok.
○ Always stir-fry the recipe ingredients in the correct order, for instance garlic, spring onions, ginger and herbs should be tackled first. Vegetables and meats should be stir-fried separately and then all the ingredients brought together for a final stir-fry and seasoning.
○ Before cooking shellfish, place a small chunk of fresh ginger in the hot oil and leave for half a minute or so before discarding. This should not only enhance the flavour but also slightly mask the fishy aroma.
○ Cut all the ingredients to a similar size and shape to help give the dish an aesthetic balance.

Cooking spare ribs for a crowd

Even the meatiest spare ribs have a high bone to meat ratio but, unfortunately, far too many retail outlets are, in my opinion, guilty of selling ribs with an excessively high bone to bone ratio.

If 500 g (1 lb) of ribs is considered to be a reasonable serving, then coping with the requirements for half a dozen or more guests will use up an inordinate amount of grill space. It follows that catering for a large number of guests and choosing fairly slow-cooking ribs can present a problem. One way of easing the problem is to oven-cook the ribs first.

Marinate the ribs in the refrigerator for 12–24 hours (following one of the recipes on pages 75–6). Drain them, reserve the marinade and place them, meat side up, in roasting tins. Cook them in a preheated oven at Gas Mark 4/180°C/350°F for about 1 hour, basting occasionally with the marinade. Drain off the excess fat and keep the ribs in a cool place until you are ready to barbecue them. Finish cooking the ribs, turning and basting them as the recipe demands, for 10–15 minutes on the barbecue.

As an alternative to roasting, the ribs can be gently simmered in spiced water. Whilst not to everyone's taste (simmering does reduce the meat's natural flavour), this technique at least avoids the oven becoming well and truly coated in grease!

Place the ribs in a large saucepan and cover with cold water. Add a bouquet garni, 2 or 3 garlic cloves and salt and pepper, to help maintain the flavour of the meat. Bring the water to the boil, simmer gently for 30–40 minutes, drain well and keep covered in the refrigerator until required. Finish cooking the ribs on the barbecue for 10 minutes or so.

Spare ribs, chops, etc. in a rib rack

Gas barbecues that have a deep lid and a reasonably large grill area, should be able to accommodate a rib rack. This useful accessory (see above), normally available in two sizes, enables the barbecue to cope with considerably more flat foods, such as spare ribs and chops, than usual. A further advantage is that the meat, being held upright, can be basted on each side, and as it is cooked by the indirect heat method it does not have to be turned continually. Spare ribs cooked in complete or multi-rib sections this way shrink less, are more succulent than single ribs and can be sliced apart easily when cooked. By using the barbecue's warming grill fully after following the pre-cooking techniques already described, it is possible to feed a large number of people.

Apart from using the direct and indirect cooking methods, a complete rib section can be spit-roasted. The spit rod should be guided through the meaty portion every two or three ribs, concertina fashion, and the whole rib section firmly secured with the meat tines. Spit roasting is not, however, a method that will substantially increase the barbecue's capacity to handle larger than normal quantities.

Cooking vegetables in foil

Happily most vegetables take kindly to being grilled directly over moderate heat; two good examples of this are Mixed Vegetable Kebabs (page 106) and Orange and Ginger Glazed Carrots (page 102). Two obvious exceptions are shelled beans and peas! Apart from stir-frying, or impaling on a fine skewer, the perfect solution when placing small or sectioned vegetables on a barbecue is to wrap them in foil. Steam-cooking vegetables in a foil package (for that is what the method really is) provides three benefits:

(a) the vegetables retain more of their natural colour;

(b) the vegetables retain a great deal of their natural flavour (unlike pot-boiled vegetables where some of the flavour, and the odd vitamin, disappear with the discarded water);

(c) the cook, having discarded the used foil, can relax in the knowledge that he or she does not have to tackle a collection of dirty pans after the meal!

Select 'heavy-duty' (extra-thick) aluminium foil for wrapping the vegetables. If you only have thin foil, use two or three layers. To be practical, I suggest you limit individual packs to three or four standard portions. Smallish packs can be accommodated more easily around a joint when cooking by the indirect heat method, especially if the barbecue is small. A piece of foil roughly 30 cm (12 inches) square should be sufficient for the purpose.

Clean and prepare the vegetables in the normal manner and pile them in the centre of the foil. Incidentally, leave the vegetables wet as the water aids the 'steam-cooking' process. Lift the edges of the foil square and add the recommended amount of water – 1 or 2 tablespoons is usually adequate. Some people prefer to add a knob of butter (plain or flavoured) or margarine instead of the water.

If you wish to cook the vegetables by the indirect heat method, I suggest you adopt the 'bundle wrapping' technique. Bring the four corners of the foil square together to form a rough pyramid shape and fold the open edges to close them and help retain the hot moist air. Try not to crush the package and remember to keep it upright! 'Bundle-wrapping' lends itself particularly well to irregularly shaped vegetables.

Cooking prepared vegetables over direct heat means that the foil package is turned frequently, so make it as leakproof as possible to avoid losing precious juices. The technique to adopt is sometimes referred to as 'drugstore wrapping' (an Americanism that does not bear translation to 'chemist shop wrapping'!). Place the prepared vegetables in the centre of a square or oblong piece of heavy-duty aluminium foil, bring the two opposite sides together above the food and turn down the edges in tight folds, leaving adequate space above the vegetables for heat expansion. Seal the open ends of the package with tight folds. The result is a neater and more water-tight version of the 'bundle wrapping' technique.

In past years I was an advocate of wrapping the vegetables with the shiny side of the foil in. I have now concluded that it doesn't matter which side is in.

Cooking times and heat settings

Many of the following recipes use the indirect heat method of cooking (the broad equivalent of roasting and baking in a domestic oven) and are based on the use of a twin burner gas barbecue rated at 33,000 BTUs (9.7 kilowatts) with a cooking area of 2090 square cm (324 square inches). This power and capacity rating is about the average for most twin burner units presently available: they range from 25,000 to 44,000 BTUs (7.3 to 13 kilowatts). Follow the variable heat settings given in the recipes, but note that some of the smaller, more compact units, with a BTU or kilowatt rating at the lower end of the scale, may in practice require a *reduction* in the recommended cooking time.

The greatest influence on the quoted cooking time is the weather – a cold, gusty wind in the barbecue area will almost certainly require the control knob to be set for a higher heat or, alternatively, for the cooking time to be increased. On a hot day, with little or no breeze, the heat setting may be lowered and/or the cooking time reduced. It is easier to judge the cooking heat if the barbecue incorporates a heat indicator/thermometer in its lid (more information on this is given on page 33). The same awareness of air temperature and wind applies when grilling with the lid open. However, despite the vagaries of the weather, it should not take long to become familiar with the cooking capabilities of a gas barbecue.

Appetisers

Bruschetta

Bruschetta (the original Italian garlic bread) makes a delicious and inexpensive appetiser, as long as all your guests like garlic!

SERVES 4

1 FRENCH BREAD STICK

4 LARGE GARLIC CLOVES (USE 1 GARLIC CLOVE FOR EVERY 2–3 SLICES OF BREAD)

EXTRA-VIRGIN OLIVE OIL

SALT AND FRESHLY GROUND BLACK PEPPER

Preheat and prepare the barbecue for grilling, following the instructions on page 30. Cut the bread into thick slices and toast directly on the grill over high heat.

Rub one side of the warm, toasted bread with the garlic (impale the garlic on a fork if you wish to avoid garlicky fingers). Drizzle plenty of olive oil over the bread and season to taste with salt and pepper.

Hot garlic bread

Remember to have paper serviettes or kitchen paper to protect buttery fingers.

SERVES 6–8

1 FRENCH BREAD STICK ABOUT 40 cm (16 INCHES) LONG

1 QUANTITY OF GARLIC BUTTER (PAGE 133), SOFTENED

Preheat and prepare the barbecue for grilling, following the instructions on page 30.

Cut the stick diagonally at 2.5 cm (1-inch) intervals almost through to the bottom. Place the stick on a sheet of heavy-duty aluminium foil and spread all the cut and outer surfaces with the Garlic Butter.

4
THE FOOD

Wrap the foil securely around the stick and heat over medium to high heat for 12–15 minutes, turning once. Cut through the bottom of the loaf to separate the slices and serve hot.

Spicy potato slices

Pictured on page 50
One of the tastiest, and certainly one of the cheapest, appetisers around.

SERVES 4–6

MAKES ABOUT 40

4 LARGE BAKING POTATOES

75 g (3 oz) BUTTER, SOFTENED

1 TABLESPOON BARBECUE SPICE

½ TEASPOON GARLIC SALT

Preheat and prepare the barbecue for grilling, following the instructions on page 30.

Cut the potatoes lengthways into slices about 3–5 mm (⅛–¼ inch) thick, discarding the outer slices. Dry the slices with kitchen paper.

Mix together the butter, barbecue spice and garlic salt.

Place the potato slices on the grill and brush generously with the spicy butter. Turn the slices over and grill, over high heat, for 4–5 minutes. Baste the uncooked sides generously, turn over and grill for a further 4–5 minutes or until the potato slices feel soft when pierced with a skewer. Serve immediately.

To serve individual slices as an appetiser, pierce the edge of each slice with two wooden cocktail sticks, roughly 1 cm (½ inch) apart. Bring the ends of the sticks together to hold and eat the slice.

Scallop and mushroom teriyaki

MAKES 12

12 SCALLOPS OUT OF THEIR SHELLS, WASHED AND DRIED

4 TABLESPOONS SOY SAUCE

40 g (1½ oz) SOFT BROWN SUGAR

2 TABLESPOONS GROUNDNUT OR SUNFLOWER OIL

1 TABLESPOON MIRIN (SWEET RICE WINE) OR DRY SHERRY

1 TEASPOON FRESHLY GRATED ROOT GINGER OR A PINCH OF GROUND GINGER

1 GARLIC CLOVE, CRUSHED

12 CLOSED-CUP MUSHROOMS, STALKS REMOVED

Preheat and prepare the barbecue for grilling, following the instructions on page 30.

Place the scallops in a bowl. Mix together the soy sauce, sugar, oil, mirin or sherry, ginger and garlic. Pour the mixture over the scallops, stir gently to coat and leave them to marinate for about 10 minutes. Remove the scallops, reserving the marinade.

Place a scallop in each mushroom cup and thread them on to skewers, taking care that the scallops are held securely. Grill, over medium to high heat, for about 5 minutes or until the scallops are opaque and firm. Turn and baste frequently with the reserved marinade. Serve immediately.

Prawn and vegetable kebabs

Pictured on the front cover

SERVES 6

24 RAW DUBLIN BAY OR PACIFIC PRAWNS, PEELED AND DE-VEINED

24 BUTTON MUSHROOMS

2 LARGE GREEN PEPPERS, EACH DE-SEEDED AND CUT INTO 12 EVEN-SIZE PIECES

12 SLICES OF LEAN BACON, EACH CUT IN HALF LENGTHWAYS

MARINADE

1 LARGE GARLIC CLOVE, CRUSHED

1 TEASPOON SALT

¼ TEASPOON FRESHLY GROUND BLACK PEPPER

1 TEASPOON CHILLI POWDER

1 TABLESPOON RED OR WHITE WINE VINEGAR

1 TEASPOON DRIED BASIL

1½ TABLESPOONS CHOPPED FRESH MINT OR 1 ROUNDED TEASPOON DRIED MINT

150 ml (¼ PINT) OIL

To make the marinade, mix together all the ingredients in a large bowl. Add the prawns, mushrooms and green peppers and turn until well coated with the marinade. Cover the bowl and refrigerate for at least 5 hours or overnight.

Soak some bamboo skewers if using. Preheat and prepare the barbecue for grilling, following the instructions on page 30.

Drain the prawns, mushrooms and peppers and reserve the marinade. Wrap half a slice of bacon around each prawn and thread on to skewers, alternating with the mushrooms and peppers. Leave a small gap each side to ensure even cooking. Cook over medium heat for 6–8 minutes until the bacon starts to crisp, turning and basting frequently with the marinade. Do not overcook. Serve hot, with any remaining marinade if wished.

Prawns with a hint of mint and garlic

Served hot from the grill these flavourful prawns make delicious appetisers.

SERVES 6–8

MAKES ABOUT 60

1 kg (2 lb) MEDIUM-SIZE RAW PRAWNS, PEELED AND DE-VEINED

MARINADE

1 LARGE OR 2 MEDIUM-SIZE GARLIC CLOVES, CRUSHED

1½ TABLESPOONS CHOPPED FRESH MINT OR 1 ROUNDED TEASPOON DRIED MINT

1 TEASPOON SALT

¼ TEASPOON FRESHLY GROUND BLACK PEPPER

1 TEASPOON CHILLI POWDER

1 TABLESPOON RED OR WHITE WINE VINEGAR

1 TEASPOON DRIED BASIL

150 ml (¼ PINT) OIL

To make the marinade, mix together the ingredients in a bowl. Add the prawns and turn until well coated with the marinade. Cover and refrigerate for 5–7 hours or overnight.

Preheat and prepare the barbecue for grilling, following the instructions on page 30.

Briefly drain the prawns and reserve the marinade. Thread the prawns on to skewers and place on the grill. Cook over medium heat for 6–8 minutes, turning once and basting frequently with the marinade. Serve hot.

Spicy grilled prawns

Pictured on page 50

SERVES 6–8

MAKES ABOUT 60

1 kg (2 lb) MEDIUM-SIZE RAW PRAWNS, PEELED AND
DE-VEINED

3½ TABLESPOONS MELTED BUTTER OR MARGARINE

MARINADE

1 TEASPOON SALT

½ TEASPOON FRESHLY GROUND BLACK PEPPER

½ TEASPOON GARLIC POWDER

4 TABLESPOONS CHILLI SAUCE

4 TABLESPOONS RED OR WHITE WINE VINEGAR

2 TABLESPOONS WORCESTERSHIRE SAUCE

4 TABLESPOONS FINELY CHOPPED FRESH PARSLEY

3½ TABLESPOONS OIL

To make the marinade, mix the ingredients in a bowl and blend well. Add the prawns and turn until completely coated with the marinade. Cover the bowl and refrigerate for 1–3 hours.

Preheat and prepare the barbecue for grilling, following the instructions on page 30.

Drain the prawns and reserve the marinade. Blend the reserved marinade with the melted butter or margarine. Thread the prawns on to skewers and place them on the grill. Cook over medium heat for 6–8 minutes, turning once and basting the prawns frequently and generously with the marinade mixture during cooking. Do not overcook the prawns as this will make them chewy.

Olive bacon titbits

MAKES 24

12 SLICES OF STREAKY BACON

24 LARGE GREEN OLIVES, STONED

Soak bamboo skewers or wooden cocktail sticks in water, if using. Preheat and prepare the barbecue for grilling, following the instructions on page 30.

Cut the bacon slices in half and grill until partially cooked but still flexible. Wrap each olive in a piece of bacon and thread it on to a fine metal or bamboo skewer. Alternatively, secure each bacon-wrapped olive with a wooden cocktail stick.

Grill over medium to high heat for about 10 minutes or until the bacon is crisp and nicely browned. Turn the titbits occasionally during cooking.

Chicken wings with honey glaze

Pictured on page 50

Cooking wing pieces in this quantity is easier if you use a large, hinged wire broiler. Remember to oil the inside of the broiler before placing the chicken pieces in it.

MAKES 40

20 MEATY CHICKEN WINGS

1 QUANTITY OF SOY SAKE MARINADE (PAGE 129)

Cut the wings through the joints and discard the bony tips. Place the chicken pieces in a large bowl and pour over the marinade. Cover and leave for 2–3 hours at room temperature or overnight in a refrigerator (turning the pieces occasionally, if possible).

Preheat and prepare the barbecue for grilling, following the instructions on page 30.

Drain the chicken pieces and reserve the marinade. Grill the pieces over medium to high heat for about 15 minutes or until cooked and a dark mahogany colour. Baste the chicken pieces frequently during the final few minutes of cooking.

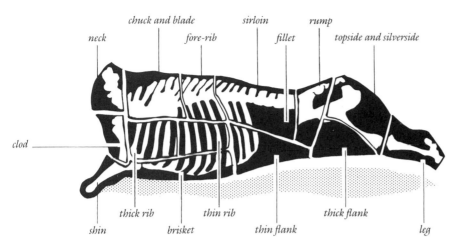

neck

chuck and blade

fore-rib

sirloin

fillet

rump

topside and silverside

clod

thick rib

shin

brisket

thin rib

thin flank

thick flank

leg

Cuts of beef

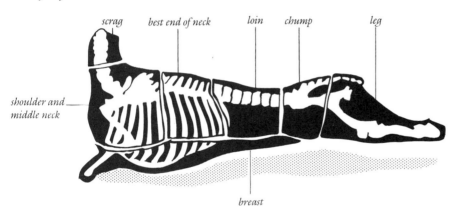

scrag

best end of neck

loin

chump

leg

shoulder and middle neck

breast

Cuts of lamb

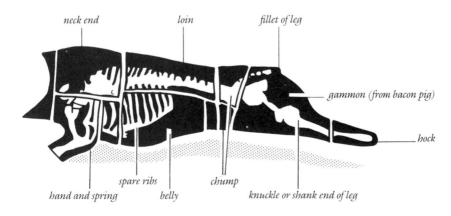

neck end

loin

fillet of leg

gammon (from bacon pig)

hock

hand and spring

spare ribs

belly

chump

knuckle or shank end of leg

Cuts of pork

Cuts
of
meat

Beef & veal

Teriyaki beef strips

SERVES 6–8

1 kg (2 lb) SIRLOIN STEAK 2 cm (¾ INCH) THICK, CUT
INTO 6 mm (¼-INCH) THICK SLICES

OIL FOR GREASING

MARINADE

6 TABLESPOONS SOY OR SHOYU SAUCE

2 TABLESPOONS DRY RED WINE, RED WINE VINEGAR
OR SAKE

1 TEASPOON GROUND GINGER

1½ TABLESPOONS OIL

1 GARLIC CLOVE, CHOPPED VERY FINELY

1–3 TEASPOONS BROWN SUGAR, TO TASTE

To make the marinade, mix together the
ingredients in a bowl. Add the meat strips
and turn until well coated with the
marinade. Cover the bowl and place in the
refrigerator for 3–4 hours.

Preheat and prepare the barbecue for
grilling, following the instructions on
page 30.

Lift the meat from the bowl, drain
briefly and reserve the marinade.

Thread the meat, snake-fashion, on to
15–20 cm (6–8-inch) long, oiled skewers.
Grill the meat over medium to high heat for
just 1–2 minutes on each side, basting once
or twice with the marinade. Avoid overcooking the meat and serve immediately.

Aloha burgers

Because of its 'arresting' nature (the spicy
beef and juicy pineapple combine nicely), I
was tempted to give this recipe the title
'aloha-aloha' and dedicate it to my friends in
the constabulary.

SERVES 6

750 g (1½ lb) LEAN MINCED BEEF

1 TEASPOON SALT

¼ TEASPOON FRESHLY GROUND BLACK PEPPER

2 TEASPOONS SOY SAUCE

6 SLICES OF CANNED PINEAPPLE, PLUS 2
TABLESPOONS JUICE

50 g (2 oz) BROWN SUGAR

1 TEASPOON WORCESTERSHIRE SAUCE

6 TABLESPOONS TOMATO KETCHUP

Preheat and prepare the barbecue for
grilling, following the instructions on
page 30.

Mix together the minced beef, salt,
pepper and soy sauce in a large bowl. Shape
the mixture into 6 burgers slightly larger in
diameter than the pineapple slices. Press a
pineapple slice into the surface of each
burger and mould the meat around it to
hold the slice firmly in place.

Place the pineapple juice, sugar,
Worcestershire sauce and tomato ketchup in
a small saucepan and heat gently for a few
minutes. Brush the hot sauce over the
pineapple surface of the burger. Grill, over
medium to high heat, for about 10 minutes,
or until the meat is done. Brush the burgers
frequently with the sauce during cooking to
give a glaze to the pineapple slices.

Steak au poivre flambé

Pictured on the front cover
This recipe provides the cook with a
wonderful opportunity to squeeze some
extra theatre and excitement from his, or
her, barbecuing efforts.

SERVES 4

2 TABLESPOONS BLACK PEPPERCORNS, CRUSHED
COARSELY

4 FILLET OR RUMP STEAKS ABOUT 2.5 cm (1 INCH)
THICK

50 g (2 oz) BUTTER

2 LARGE TOMATOES, SLICED THICKLY

A PINCH OF FRESH OR DRIED OREGANO

A PINCH OF GARLIC SALT

4 TABLESPOONS BRANDY

Press the peppercorns firmly into both sides
of the meat. Leave the steaks at room
temperature for 30–40 minutes.

Preheat and prepare the barbecue for
grilling, following the instructions on
page 30.

Grill the meat over high heat until
cooked to the desired degree (about 5
minutes per side for rare). When cooked,
transfer the meat to a hot, shallow dish.

Melt the butter in a frying pan, add the
tomato slices and heat through. Season with
the oregano and garlic salt. Arrange the
tomato slices on top of the steaks. Warm the
brandy, spoon it evenly over the steaks and
ignite. Serve as soon as the flames subside.

Stuffed rump steak with tarragon and parsley butter

SERVES 4

750 g (1½ lb) RUMP STEAK, CUT ABOUT 4 cm
(1½ INCHES) THICK

1 QUANTITY OF TARRAGON AND PARSLEY BUTTER
(PAGE 134), CHILLED

OIL FOR BRUSHING

STUFFING

1 TEASPOON FINELY CHOPPED SHALLOT OR ONION

A LITTLE OIL

125 g (4 oz) OPEN MUSHROOMS, CHOPPED FINELY

1 TEASPOON FINELY CHOPPED FRESH PARSLEY

1 GARLIC CLOVE, CRUSHED

1 ROUNDED TABLESPOON FINELY CHOPPED COOKED
HAM

1 TABLESPOON FRESH BREADCRUMBS

SALT AND FRESHLY GROUND BLACK PEPPER

To prepare the stuffing, in a pan cook the
shallot or onion in a little oil until soft. Add
the mushrooms, parsley and garlic, cover the
pan and cook, over medium heat, for about
5 minutes. Add the ham, breadcrumbs and
salt and pepper and stir lightly to mix. Turn
the mixture on to a plate to cool.

Preheat and prepare the barbecue for
grilling, following the instructions on
page 30.

Slit the steak on one side to form a deep
pocket. Push the stuffing well into the
pocket and close the opening with a trussing
needle and string or a fine skewer.

Slice the butter into pats.

Brush the steak with oil and grill, over
medium to high heat, for about 4–5 minutes
on each side, or until cooked to the desired
degree. Remove the string or skewer.

Cut the steak into 1 cm (½-inch) thick
slices and serve with the flavoured butter.

Stir-fried steak in oyster sauce

SERVES 4–6

750 g (1½ lb) RUMP OR FILLET BEEF STEAK, SLICED THINLY

1 TABLESPOON CORNFLOUR

½ TEASPOON SALT

4 TABLESPOONS OIL

1 TABLESPOON SOY SAUCE

2 TABLESPOONS OYSTER SAUCE

½ CHICKEN STOCK CUBE, CRUSHED

2 TABLESPOONS DRY SHERRY

FRESHLY GROUND BLACK PEPPER

Preheat and prepare the barbecue for wok-cooking, following the instructions on page 38.

Cut the steak across the grain into 5 cm (2-inch) strips the thickness of a pencil. Sprinkle with the cornflour and the salt, and pepper to taste, and mix together lightly.

Place the wok on the barbecue, add the oil and, when very hot, add the beef, spreading the strips evenly. Stir-fry over high heat for 1 minute. Add the soy and oyster sauces, the crushed stock cube and the sherry. Stir-fry for a further 1 minute and then turn out on to a warmed dish.

Serve immediately, with rice or noodles.

Dr Barnes's short ribs

This recipe, selected for its strong 'bones' association, is dedicated to friend and fellow barbecue *aficionado* Dr Ron Barnes. Ron regularly creates many delicacies on his barbecue, including the tastiest seafood kebabs this side of the Atlantic.

SERVES 4–6

1.25 kg (3 lb) LEAN SHORT RIBS (CUT FROM FORE-RIB OF BEEF)

MARINADE

150 ml (¼ PINT) DRY RED WINE

1 TABLESPOON WORCESTERSHIRE SAUCE

1 TABLESPOON SOY SAUCE

300 ml (½ PINT) TOMATO JUICE

2 GARLIC CLOVES, CHOPPED VERY FINELY

¼ TEASPOON GROUND CLOVES

1 TEASPOON MUSTARD POWDER

¼ TEASPOON DRIED THYME

1 TABLESPOON BROWN SUGAR

1 TEASPOON SALT

1 SMALL ONION, CHOPPED FINELY

3 TABLESPOONS OIL

Place the ribs in a shallow dish. Combine all the marinade ingredients, except the onion and oil, and pour over the meat. Cover the dish and place in the refrigerator for 24–48 hours, turning the ribs occasionally.

Leave the meat at room temperature for 2–3 hours before cooking. About 30 minutes before cooking the ribs, add the onion and oil to the marinade and stir the mixture well.

Preheat and prepare the barbecue for grilling, following the instructions on page 30.

Lightly drain the ribs and reserve the marinade. Place the ribs on the grill(s) and cook for 30–40 minutes, or until done to your liking. Turn and baste the ribs with the marinade every 5–10 minutes. Serve with any leftover marinade, if wished.

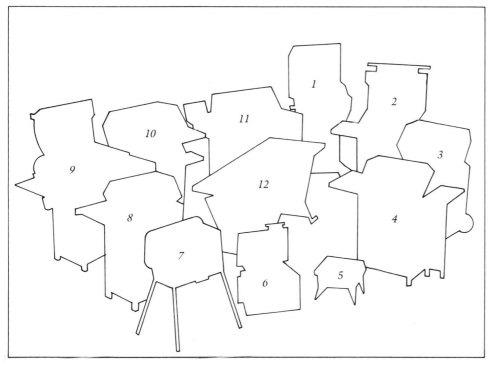

1. Large wagon gas barbecue with rotisserie burner;
2. Wagon gas barbecue;
3. Wagon gas barbecue;
4. Small wagon gas barbecue;
5. Fully portable gas barbecue;
6. Fully portable gas barbecue;
7. Portable 'briefcase' gas barbecue; 8. Portable gas barbecue in removable cart;
9. Large wagon gas barbecue;
10. Large wagon gas barbecue;
11. Large wagon gas barbecue with side burner;
12. Portable commercial catering gas barbecue

Spicy
potato slices
Page 42

Chicken wings
with honey glaze
Page 44

Spicy
grilled prawns
Page 44

*Hot 'n' spicy
bumper burger*
Page 54

*Red wine
burgers*
Page 54

Barbecued
Boeuf en croûte
Page 57

Skewered
veal and
ham olives
Page 58

Steak with blue cheese butter

SERVES 4–6

750 g (1½ lb) WHOLE FLANK STEAK

175 ml (6 fl oz) FRENCH DRESSING

1 TABLESPOON SOFT BUTTER

75 g (3 oz) BLUE CHEESE

1 TABLESPOON FINELY CHOPPED CHIVES

1 GARLIC CLOVE, CHOPPED VERY FINELY

1 TABLESPOON CHOPPED FRESH ROSEMARY OR 1
TEASPOON DRIED ROSEMARY

A PINCH OF DRIED OREGANO OR DRIED BASIL

A PINCH OF FRESHLY GROUND BLACK PEPPER

Place the steak in a shallow dish and pour over the french dressing. Turn the steak 2 or 3 times; then cover the dish and place in the refrigerator for at least 4 hours or overnight.

Blend together the butter, blue cheese, chives, garlic, rosemary and oregano or basil. Add a pinch of freshly ground black pepper. Chill if not using immediately.

Preheat and prepare the barbecue for grilling, following the instructions on page 30.

Lift the steak from the dish and drain briefly. Grill over high heat for about 4–5 minutes per side – depending on the thickness of the steak. For best eating the steak should be served rare (medium and well-done flank usually ends up being rather tough).

Place the steak on a warm platter, slice it thinly across the grain at an angle of 45 degrees and serve with a pat or spoonful of the blue cheese butter on each portion.

Teriyaki flank steak

This recipe is best made with thick flank, so request this specially from your butcher. And remember, hot or cold teriyaki flank steak sandwiches are hard to beat.

SERVES 4–6

750 g (1½ lb) WHOLE FLANK STEAK

MARINADE

6 TABLESPOONS SOY SAUCE

150 ml (¼ PINT) RED WINE OR RED WINE VINEGAR

2 TEASPOONS FRESHLY GRATED ROOT GINGER OR ½
TEASPOON GROUND GINGER

1 GARLIC CLOVE, CHOPPED VERY FINELY OR
CRUSHED

2 TABLESPOONS BROWN SUGAR, PACKED FIRMLY

2 TABLESPOONS LEMON JUICE

2 TABLESPOONS OIL

1 MEDIUM-SIZE ONION, CHOPPED FINELY

¼ TEASPOON FRESHLY GROUND BLACK PEPPER

Give the steak a good beating with a rolling pin or wooden steak hammer. Place the steak in a shallow dish.

Mix together all the ingredients for the marinade and pour over the meat. Cover and leave in the refrigerator for at least 6 hours or overnight.

Preheat and prepare the barbecue for grilling, following the instructions on page 30.

Lift the steak from the marinade, drain briefly and reserve the marinade. Place the steak on the grill and cook, over high heat, for about 5 minutes each side, basting occasionally with the marinade. (Flank should only be served rare for, despite marinating, 'medium to well-done' steaks usually become tough.)

To serve the steak, slice it thinly at an angle of 45 degrees.

Hot 'n' spicy bumper burger

Pictured on page 51

A giant burger that provides eight people with something worth getting their teeth into.

SERVES 8

1 ROUND BREAD COB ABOUT 25 cm (10 INCHES) IN DIAMETER, OR 2 PITTA BREADS

1 QUANTITY OF GARLIC BUTTER OR TARRAGON AND PARSLEY BUTTER (PAGE 133 OR 134), AT ROOM TEMPERATURE

1 kg (2 lb) CHUCK STEAK, MINCED FINELY

1 LARGE ONION, CHOPPED FINELY

½ TEASPOON MUSTARD POWDER

1 TABLESPOON SOY SAUCE

1 TABLESPOON CHILLI SAUCE

2 TEASPOONS HORSERADISH SAUCE

¼ TEASPOON GROUND GINGER

1 TABLESPOON WORCESTERSHIRE SAUCE

OIL FOR GREASING, IF NECESSARY

TO SERVE

1 LARGE RED ONION, SLICED THINLY (OPTIONAL)

2 LARGE TOMATOES, SLICED THINLY

1 AVOCADO, SLICED THINLY

SHREDDED LETTUCE

Slice the cob in half horizontally. If pitta bread is used, part-slice these horizontally and lift open to make a large, hinged flat bread. Spread the cut surfaces of either bread with the flavoured butter.

In a large bowl mix together the meat, onion, mustard, soy sauce, chilli sauce, horseradish sauce, ginger and Worcester-shire sauce. Shape the mixture into one large burger slightly bigger in diameter than the cob or opened out pitta bread.

Preheat and prepare the barbecue for grilling, following the instructions on page 30.

Oil a large, hinged broiler and place the burger inside. Alternatively, place the burger directly on the grill. Cook the burger over high heat for 6–10 minutes per side or until cooked to the desired degree. If cooking directly on the grill, use 2 rimless baking sheets – one slipped under the burger and one on top – to turn the burger. Once turned, place the bread, cut side down, to toast on the grill.

To garnish and serve, place the burger on the bottom half of the cob, or on one of the pitta breads, and top with the onion slices (if used), tomato slices, avocado slices, shredded lettuce and remaining bread. Cut into 8 equal-size wedges and serve immediately.

Red wine burgers

Pictured on page 51

SERVES 6–8

50 g (2 oz) BUTTER

2 MEDIUM-SIZE ONIONS, CHOPPED FINELY

5 TABLESPOONS DRY RED WINE

750 g (1½ lb) FINELY MINCED CHUCK STEAK

40 g (1½ oz) FRESH BREADCRUMBS

1 TEASPOON SALT

¼ TEASPOON FRESHLY GROUND BLACK PEPPER

1 EGG, BEATEN

6–8 SOFT ROLLS

Preheat and prepare the barbecue for grilling, following the instructions on page 30.

Place half the butter, onion and red wine on one side.

Lightly mix the remaining wine, butter and onion into the meat. Stir in the breadcrumbs, salt, pepper and egg. Shape the mixture into 6–8 burgers approximately 2 cm (¾ inch) thick.

Melt the reserved butter in a small saucepan, add the reserved onion and fry gently until transparent. Add the reserved wine and simmer for about 5 minutes.

Brush the wine sauce over the burgers and grill, over medium to high heat, for about 8–10 minutes each side. Brush the sauce over the burgers occasionally during cooking. Toast the rolls during the last few minutes of cooking.

Fill the rolls with the burgers, garnish if wished and serve.

Fill the meat shells with the onion mixture and sprinkle over the grated cheese. Cook the meat tarts until the cheese melts, closing the barbecue lid to help melt the cheese. (The meat tarts can be cooked throughout with the lid closed, if wished.)

Carefully remove the meat tarts from the foil moulds and serve.

Grilled meat tarts with mushroom and onion filling

SERVES 6

750 g (1½ lb) LEAN BEEF, MINCED FINELY

3 TABLESPOONS FINE DRY BREADCRUMBS

1 EGG

2 TABLESPOONS SOFT BUTTER

1 TABLESPOON FINELY CHOPPED ONION

250 g (8 oz) CLOSED-CUP MUSHROOMS, SLICED

75 g (3 oz) GRATED CHEDDAR CHEESE

SALT AND FRESHLY GROUND BLACK PEPPER

Preheat and prepare the barbecue for grilling, following the instructions on page 30.

Place the minced beef, breadcrumbs, ½ teaspoon of salt, ¼ teaspoon of pepper and egg in a bowl and blend carefully. Divide the mixture into 6 equal portions. Form each portion into a 1 cm (½-inch) thick patty about 10 cm (4 inches) in diameter. Lightly press each patty into an aluminium foil individual tart mould, covering the bottom and sides.

Place the moulds upside-down on the grill and cook, over medium heat, until the meat just starts to turn brown. Take care not to overcook the meat or it will become dry.

While the meat is cooking, melt the butter in a small pan and cook the onion until just golden. Add the mushrooms, season to taste and cook until soft.

Beef and courgette kebabs

Pictured on the front cover

SERVES 4

1 kg (2 lb) RUMP, SIRLOIN OR FILLET STEAK

2 COURGETTES

3 TABLESPOONS GROUNDNUT OIL

3 TABLESPOONS SOFT BUTTER

1 GARLIC CLOVE, CRUSHED

¼ TEASPOON FRESHLY GROUND BLACK PEPPER

4 MEDIUM-SIZE TOMATOES, QUARTERED

Trim the meat and cut into 2.5 cm (1-inch) cubes.

Slice the courgettes into circles about 1 cm (½ inch) thick. Blanch them in a pan of boiling water for 30 seconds. Drain well.

Preheat and prepare the barbecue for grilling, following the instructions on page 30.

Place the oil, butter, garlic and pepper in a small saucepan and heat gently for a few minutes. Keep the pan on the side of the grill for basting.

Thread the meat cubes, courgette slices and tomato pieces alternately on to skewers and brush with the garlic oil.

Grill over medium to high heat, turning and basting frequently, for about 10 minutes or until cooked to the desired degree.

T-bone with rosemary

SERVES 4–6

1 T-BONE STEAK, 4–5 cm (1½–2 INCHES) THICK

1 TABLESPOON OIL

2 TABLESPOONS CHOPPED FRESH ROSEMARY OR 2 TEASPOONS DRIED ROSEMARY

SALT AND FRESHLY GROUND BLACK PEPPER

Brush the meat all over with the oil and press equal portions of the rosemary into both sides. Leave it at room temperature for about 30 minutes.

Preheat and prepare the barbecue for indirect heat cooking, following the instructions on page 33.

Roast the meat with medium heat until cooked to the desired degree (about 15 minutes each side for rare meat). Turn over the meat, carefully, half-way through cooking.

Season with salt and pepper and cut the meat across the grain in thin slanting slices to serve.

Roast sirloin with sesame

SERVES 6–8

1.5–2 kg (3½–4½ lb) SIRLOIN OF BEEF

MARINADE

4 TABLESPOONS SESAME SEEDS

6 TABLESPOONS SOY SAUCE

6 TABLESPOONS OIL

4 TABLESPOONS LEMON JUICE, STRAINED

2 TABLESPOONS WHITE WINE VINEGAR

1 MEDIUM-SIZE ONION, CHOPPED FINELY

2 GARLIC CLOVES, CHOPPED VERY FINELY OR CRUSHED

1 TABLESPOON SUGAR

To make the marinade, heat a small saucepan over medium heat. Add the sesame seeds and, turning occasionally, cook until they are golden brown. Remove the pan from the heat and add the soy sauce, oil, lemon juice, vinegar, onion, garlic and sugar.

Put the meat in a baking dish and pour the marinade over to coat it. Cover the dish with clingfilm. Leave the meat to marinate in the refrigerator overnight, or even for a full day, turning the meat occasionally.

Preheat and prepare the barbecue for indirect heat cooking, following the instructions on page 33.

Remove the meat from the marinade and drain briefly. Reserve the marinade.

Roast the meat with medium heat until cooked to the desired degree – cooked rare this would be about 1½ hours for a 2 kg (4½ lb) joint or until a meat thermometer inserted into the centre of the roast registers 60°C/140°F. During cooking, baste the meat occasionally with the reserved marinade.

Allow the meat to rest for about 15 minutes before carving.

Barbecued boeuf en croûte

Pictured on page 52

Boeuf en Croûte (Beef Wellington) is a spectacular dish to present to your friends, and although on the expensive side, it is relatively easy to prepare. Apart from beef, cooking *en croûte* can be applied to boned venison, lamb, chicken or large fish such as salmon and sea trout.

Although I suggest the preparation is done the day before, it can be carried out on the day, providing the part-cooked meat is quite cold and the pastry well chilled before completing the dish.

SERVES 6

1 kg (2 lb) FILLET OF BEEF

BRANDY FOR BRUSHING

75 g (3 oz) BUTTER

1 SPANISH ONION, CHOPPED FINELY

250 g (8 oz) CLOSED-CUP BUTTON MUSHROOMS, CHOPPED FINELY

2 TEASPOONS CHOPPED MIXED FRESH HERBS

500 g (1 lb) PACKET OF PUFF PASTRY, CHILLED WELL

1 EGG, BEATEN WELL

A LITTLE RED WINE

SALT AND FRESHLY GROUND BLACK PEPPER

FRESH WATERCRESS OR PARSLEY, TO GARNISH

The day before, preheat the oven to Gas Mark 7/220°C/425°F.

Trim any excess fat from the fillet and tie it into a compact shape. Brush the fillet generously with brandy.

Melt 25 g (1 oz) of the butter in a roasting tin. Increase the heat, add the meat and brown it quickly all over. Then roast the meat in the oven for 15 minutes, basting it occasionally with the pan juices.

Remove the meat from the oven and allow it to get cold. Remove the string and place the meat in the refrigerator. Reserve the pan juices for making gravy.

The next day, melt the remaining butter in a small saucepan, add the onion and cook for about 5 minutes. Add the mushrooms and mixed herbs and continue cooking over a gentle heat until the mixture is fairly concentrated (this takes about 20 minutes). Season the mixture with salt and pepper and put on one side to cool.

Preheat and prepare the barbecue for indirect heat cooking, following the instructions on page 33.

Roll out the pastry to a rectangle about 38 × 25 cm (15 × 10 inches). Reserve the edge trimmings for decoration.

Spread half the mushroom mixture over the centre of the pastry and place the meat on top. Spread the remaining mushroom mixture over the fillet. Brush the edge of the pastry with some of the beaten egg and wrap the pastry around the fillet, pressing the edges together firmly. Brush any excess pastry at the ends with more of the egg and double-fold. Cut out diamond shapes from the reserved pastry, moisten with more of the beaten egg and use to decorate the pastry. Brush the pastry all over with the rest of the egg.

Carefully place the pastry-wrapped beef on a baking sheet and bake with medium to high heat for 35–40 minutes, or until the pastry is well browned.

Add some red wine to the reserved pan juices and simmer to reduce slightly. Keep warm.

Cut the beef into thick slices and serve it garnished with watercress or parsley, with the gravy.

Skewered veal and ham olives

Pictured on page 52

This dish can also be made using escalopes of pork. I personally like the strong scent and flavour from the sage but, if preferred, use leaves of basil or mint.

SERVES 4

4 VEAL ESCALOPES, CUT INTO THIN 10–13 cm (4–5-INCH) SQUARES

LEMON JUICE TO TASTE

4 THIN SLICES OF COOKED HAM, CUT INTO 10–13 cm (4–5 INCH) SQUARES

4 RASHERS OF STREAKY BACON, SLICED THINLY

2 MEDIUM-SIZE ONIONS, CUT INTO 5 mm (¼-INCH) THICK SLICES

SAGE LEAVES

2 TABLESPOONS MELTED BACON FAT OR DRIPPING

SALT AND FRESHLY GROUND BLACK PEPPER

Preheat and prepare the barbecue for grilling, following the instructions on page 30.

Season the veal escalopes with lemon juice and salt and pepper. Lay a slice of ham on each escalope. Roll up the meat and tightly wrap a piece of streaky bacon around each roll.

Thread two veal and ham olives on to a skewer or, preferably, two skewers spaced about 4 cm (1½ inches) apart. Do the same with the other two olives. Alternate each olive with a slice of onion and a sage leaf.

Brush the olives with the melted bacon fat or dripping and grill, over medium heat, for about 8 minutes or until cooked through. Turn and baste a few times during cooking.

Veal and streaky kebabs

SERVES 4

500 g (1 lb) LEAN SHOULDER OF VEAL OR VEAL FILLET

6 RASHERS OF STREAKY BACON

250 g (8 oz) BUTTON MUSHROOMS

1 LARGE GREEN PEPPER, DE-SEEDED, GRILLED AND SKINNED, AND CUT INTO 2.5 cm (1-INCH) SQUARES

A PINCH OF GROUND GINGER

A PINCH OF GROUND MACE

A PINCH OF GROUND NUTMEG

75 g (3 oz) BUTTER

SALT AND FRESHLY GROUND BLACK PEPPER

Preheat and prepare the barbecue for grilling, following the instructions on page 30.

Cut the veal into 2–2.5 cm (¾–1-inch) cubes. Roll up each rasher of bacon and cut in half to make 2 rolls.

Thread the bacon, veal, mushrooms and green pepper on to metal skewers, making sure that a roll of bacon is nestling against each cube of veal. Sprinkle the meat with the spices and seasonings. Dot each skewerful with the butter.

Grill, over medium heat, for about 15–20 minutes, until the bacon and veal are cooked, turning the kebabs frequently.

Stuffed veal chops

SERVES 4

4 VEAL CHOPS ABOUT 2.5 cm (1 INCH) THICK

4 VERY THIN SLICES OF BACON

4 SLICES OF GRUYÈRE OR FONTINA CHEESE

1 TABLESPOON CHOPPED FRESH THYME OR ROSEMARY

OIL FOR BRUSHING

SALT, FRESHLY GROUND BLACK PEPPER AND GRATED NUTMEG

Preheat and prepare the barbecue for grilling, following the instructions on page 30.

Cut a deep pocket, almost to the bone, through the thick part of each chop. Slide a slice of bacon and a slice of cheese into each pocket, together with a sprinkling of the chopped herbs.

Lay the chops on a board and beat the open edges hard with a rolling pin or meat hammer.

Brush the chops with oil and season with salt, pepper and grated nutmeg.

Grill the chops, over medium heat, for about 8 minutes each side or until the cheese begins to melt and run out of the chops. Serve immediately.

Roast veal

Serve this with veal forcemeat or stuffing balls and cook them alongside the roast during the last 40 minutes or so of cooking.

SERVES 6
1.75 kg (4 lb) LOIN, LEG OR SHOULDER OF VEAL, BONED AND ROLLED
FLOUR FOR SPRINKLING
8 RASHERS OF STREAKY BACON
50 g (2 oz) FAT, PREFERABLY DRIPPING
SALT AND FRESHLY GROUND BLACK PEPPER

Stand the joint in a roasting tin, sprinkle with flour and season lightly. Lay the rashers of bacon evenly over the joint and spread the fat liberally over the whole joint.

Preheat and prepare the barbecue for indirect heat cooking, following the instructions on page 33.

Roast the joint, with medium to high heat, for about 20 minutes; then lower the heat to medium for the remaining cooking. A 1.75 kg (4 lb) veal joint should take 1¾–2 hours to cook until well-done. Allow the joint 10 minutes to rest before carving.

Lamb

Lambapple burgers

SERVES 6
500 g (1 lb) MINCED LAMB
2 TABLESPOONS CHOPPED FRESH PARSLEY
A GENEROUS PINCH OF DRIED ROSEMARY
2 TEASPOONS SOY SAUCE
¼ TEASPOON SALT
A PINCH OF FRESHLY GROUND BLACK PEPPER
275 g (9 oz) CAN OF PINEAPPLE SLICES
50 g (2 oz) SOFT BROWN SUGAR
2 TEASPOONS WORCESTERSHIRE SAUCE
6 TABLESPOONS TOMATO KETCHUP

Preheat and prepare the barbecue for grilling, following the instructions on page 30.

Place the minced lamb, herbs, soy sauce and salt and pepper in a bowl and mix together. Lightly press the mixture into 6 burger shapes. Drain the pineapple slices and reserve about 2 tablespoons of the juice.

Press a pineapple slice into the surface of each burger and mould the minced meat up and around the edge of the pineapple slice.

Place the sugar, Worcestershire sauce, tomato ketchup and reserved pineapple juice in a pan and heat gently for a few minutes, stirring occasionally.

Brush the warmed sauce over the burgers and grill, over medium to high heat, for about 10 minutes or until the meat is cooked. Baste frequently with the sauce to glaze the pineapple slices and close the barbecue lid for the final two minutes or so of cooking to darken the glaze.

Turkistan kebabs

Pictured on page 69
Centuries ago, the fierce Turkish warriors used their swords to impale meat and grill it over the camp fire. Thus began the art of skewer cooking.

SERVES 6

1 kg (2 lb) LEAN BONELESS LAMB

175 g (6 oz) SUET

125 g (4 oz) ONION, CHOPPED FINELY

25 g (1 oz) FRESH PARSLEY, CHOPPED FINELY

1 GARLIC CLOVE, CHOPPED VERY FINELY

1 TEASPOON PAPRIKA

½ TEASPOON FRESHLY GROUND BLACK PEPPER

2 TEASPOONS SALT

2 TEASPOONS LEMON JUICE

2 EGGS

OIL FOR BRUSHING AND GREASING

Pass the meat and suet through the medium-size disc of a grinder. Combine the meat/suet mixture with the onion, parsley, garlic, paprika, pepper, salt and lemon juice and pass through the grinder – this time fitted with the fine disc – again. Blend thoroughly. Add the eggs and, with wet hands, mix well. Chill the mixture in the refrigerator for about 30 minutes or until firm.

Preheat and prepare the barbecue for grilling, following the instructions on page 30.

Re-wet the hands and mould the meat mixture on to oiled skewers to form torpedo-shaped pieces about 7.5 cm (3 inches) long and 2.5 cm (1 inch) in diameter.

Brush the meat with oil and grill, over high heat, for 8–10 minutes, turning to brown all sides.

Lamb satay

A lot of preparation work is required for this recipe, but the end result is very 'sataysfying'!

SERVES 6

1 kg (2 lb) FILLET END LEG OF LAMB

MARINADE

4 TABLESPOONS SOY SAUCE

3 GARLIC CLOVES, CRUSHED

1 SMALL ONION, CHOPPED FINELY

1 TABLESPOON LEMON JUICE

1 TABLESPOON SOFT BROWN SUGAR

SATAY SAUCE

2 TEASPOONS OIL

1 LARGE GARLIC CLOVE, CRUSHED

3 TABLESPOONS SMOOTH PEANUT BUTTER

1½ TABLESPOONS SOY SAUCE

2 TEASPOONS LEMON JUICE

1 GREEN OR RED CHILLI, CHOPPED FINELY

50 g (2 oz) CREAMED COCONUT

3 TABLESPOONS CHICKEN STOCK

Cut the lamb into 2.5 cm (1-inch) cubes, removing any fat or gristle.

Mix together the ingredients for the marinade in a large bowl. Add the cubes of meat and turn to coat evenly with the marinade. Cover the bowl and leave, at room temperature, for about an hour.

Preheat and prepare the barbecue for grilling, following the instructions on page 30.

Meanwhile, prepare the sauce. Heat the oil in a saucepan and cook the garlic over low heat for 1–2 minutes. Add the peanut butter and cook, stirring, until it starts to darken. Add the soy sauce, lemon juice, chilli, creamed coconut and stock and bring slowly to the boil, stirring constantly. Remove the pan to a corner of the grill or on the warming grill and allow to simmer for 5–6 minutes, stirring occasionally. Keep the sauce warm.

Lightly drain the lamb cubes, discarding the marinade, and thread on to skewers, allowing a small gap between the cubes. Cook, over high heat, for 10–15 minutes until all the sides are browned. (If you like lamb 'French-style', 10 minutes grilling should give meat that is handsomely browned outside and pink and juicy inside.)

Pour the prepared sauce into small individual warmed dishes and serve immediately, with the meat. Your guests dip the cooked meat into the sauce as they wish.

Andalusian lamb chops

<u>SERVES 6</u>

6 LAMB CHUMP CHOPS

<u>MARINADE</u>

2 TABLESPOONS FINELY CHOPPED ONION

150 ml (¼ PINT) DRY SHERRY

1 BAY LEAF

½ TEASPOON DRIED OREGANO

¾ TEASPOON DRIED BASIL

3 TABLESPOONS TARRAGON VINEGAR

6 TABLESPOONS OIL

½ TEASPOON FRESHLY GROUND BLACK PEPPER

Place the chops in a shallow dish. Mix together the marinade ingredients and pour over the meat. Cover and marinate overnight in the refrigerator, or for 4–6 hours at room temperature, turning the chops occasionally. If refrigerated, allow the meat to stand at room temperature for about an hour before cooking.

Preheat and prepare the barbecue for grilling, following the instructions on page 30.

Lightly drain the chops and reserve the marinade. Place the chops on the grill and cook, over medium to high heat, for about 10–12 minutes each side or until done to the desired degree, basting occasionally with the marinade.

Noisettes with cheese

<u>SERVES 6</u>

6 BEST END LAMB NOISETTES, CUT 2.5 cm (1 INCH) THICK

175 g (6 oz) BLUE CHEESE OR 75 g (3 oz) PARMESAN CHEESE, GRATED

50 g (2 oz) BUTTER, SOFTENED

SALT AND FRESHLY GROUND BLACK PEPPER

Preheat and prepare the barbecue for grilling, following the instructions on page 30.

Season the noisettes with salt and pepper. Grill on one side, over medium heat, for about 8 minutes.

Blend the cheese and the butter together and place on one side. Grill the other side of the noisettes for about 5 minutes and spread with the cheese mixture. Grill the meat for a further 2–3 minutes. Serve immediately.

Cinnamon lamb cutlets

<u>SERVES 6</u>

12 BEST END LAMB CUTLETS

<u>MARINADE</u>

1½ TEASPOONS GROUND CINNAMON

1 TABLESPOON BROWN SUGAR

3 TABLESPOONS OIL

6 TABLESPOONS ORANGE JUICE

¼ TEASPOON FRESHLY GROUND BLACK PEPPER

¼ TEASPOON SALT

Place the cutlets in a shallow dish. Mix together the marinade ingredients. Pour the marinade over the meat, turning it once or twice so the cutlets are well coated. Cover and marinate at room temperature for about 4 hours, or overnight in a refrigerator, turning the cutlets twice during this period.

Preheat and prepare the barbecue for grilling, following the instructions on page 30.

Briefly drain the cutlets and reserve the

marinade. Place the cutlets on the grill and cook, over medium heat, for about 25 minutes, turning and basting occasionally with the reserved marinade. Do not overcook.

Soy and ginger flavoured lamb cutlets

Teriyaki sauce is available from stores and supermarkets, or you can make your own following the recipe on page 130 (in which case you will have to omit the honey). The marinade in this recipe can also be used for chicken and pork.

SERVES 6

12 BEST END LAMB CUTLETS

MARINADE

3 TABLESPOONS OIL

1½ TABLESPOONS TERIYAKI SAUCE

1 TABLESPOON JAPANESE OR WHITE WINE VINEGAR

1 TABLESPOON DIJON WHOLE-GRAIN MUSTARD

1 SMALL PIECE OF FRESH ROOT GINGER, PEELED AND GRATED

Place the cutlets in a shallow dish. Mix together the marinade ingredients and pour over the meat. Turn the meat once or twice so that it is evenly coated. Marinate at room temperature for about 2 hours, turning the cutlets twice.

Preheat and prepare the barbecue for grilling, following the instructions on page 30.

Briefly drain the cutlets and reserve the marinade. Place on the grill and cook, over medium heat, for about 15 minutes, turning and basting occasionally with the reserved marinade.

Lemony lamb leg steaks

SERVES 4

4 × 2–2.5 cm (¾–1-INCH) THICK LAMB LEG STEAKS

MARINADE

150 ml (¼ PINT) OIL

6 TABLESPOONS LEMON JUICE

1 TEASPOON SALT

1 TEASPOON DRIED OREGANO

1 MEDIUM-SIZE ONION, CHOPPED FINELY

1 GARLIC CLOVE, CRUSHED

¼ TEASPOON FRESHLY GROUND BLACK PEPPER

GARNISH

FRESH PARSLEY

LEMON SLICES

Place the leg steaks in a shallow dish. Mix together the ingredients for the marinade and pour it over the meat. Turn the meat twice to coat well. Cover the dish and leave for at least 4 hours at room temperature, or overnight in the refrigerator. If refrigerated, allow the meat to stand at room temperature for 2–3 hours before cooking.

Preheat and prepare the barbecue for grilling, following the instructions on page 30.

Remove the leg steaks from the marinade and drain briefly. Place the steaks on the grill, over medium to high heat, and cook for 6–7 minutes on each side, or until done to your liking. Garnish the steaks with parsley and lemon slices.

Mint jelly glazed breast of lamb

A cheap, but none-the-less very tasty cut, that barbecues well. Apart from the bones, remember to remove the tough membrane.

SERVES 4

1 LARGE BONED BREAST OF LAMB WEIGHING ABOUT 750 g (1½ lb)

75 g (3 oz) FRESH WHITE BREADCRUMBS

½ TEASPOON CONCENTRATED MINT SAUCE

GRATED ZEST AND JUICE OF 1 LEMON

1 EGG, BEATEN

MINT JELLY FOR GLAZING

SALT AND FRESHLY GROUND BLACK PEPPER

CHOPPED FRESH PARSLEY TO GARNISH

Preheat and prepare the barbecue for indirect heat cooking, following the instructions on page 33.

Season the boned breast of lamb with salt and pepper.

Mix together the breadcrumbs, mint sauce, lemon zest and juice and enough of the beaten egg to make a fairly stiff mixture.

Spread the mixture evenly over the cut side of the meat. Roll up the breast tightly and secure with strong string every 2.5 cm (1 inch) along the roll.

Place on the grill and roast, with medium heat, for 1¼–1½ hours.

Spread a thin layer of mint jelly over the surface of the roll during the last 5 minutes of cooking time. Allow the meat to stand for about 10 minutes. To serve, carve the meat into thick slices and garnish with chopped parsley.

Herb and honey roast lamb

SERVES 6–8

2 BEST ENDS OF NECK OF LAMB, CHINED

3 TABLESPOONS CLEAR HONEY, WARMED

2 TABLESPOONS CHOPPED FRESH MIXED HERBS (CHOOSE FROM MINT, ROSEMARY, THYME, MARJORAM OR TARRAGON) OR 3 TEASPOONS DRIED HERBS

5 TABLESPOONS FRESH BREADCRUMBS

2 TEASPOONS GRATED LEMON ZEST

SALT AND FRESHLY GROUND BLACK PEPPER

With a sharp, short-bladed knife carefully trim the meat and fat 2.5 cm (1 inch) from the end of the rib bones on each joint.

Preheat and prepare the barbecue for indirect heat cooking, following the instructions on page 33.

Brush the surface of the lamb with the warm honey. Mix together the herbs, breadcrumbs, lemon zest and salt and pepper. Sprinkle the mixture evenly over the surface of fat.

Cook, with medium heat, for about 1¼ hours or until cooked to the desired degree. To serve, carve between the rib bones to yield 7–8 slices per best end of neck.

Butterflied leg of lamb in a herb crust

Pictured on page 70

Apart from having to remove the bone (your butcher should do this if you ask him nicely) and having to stand duty whilst the meat is cooking, this is a very good way to tackle a leg of lamb. Remember that lamb is best eaten, like a good quality beef steak, reasonably rare.

SERVES 6–8

2.25–2.75 kg (5–6 lb) LEG OF LAMB

1 TABLESPOON CHOPPED FRESH ROSEMARY OR 1 TEASPOON DRIED ROSEMARY

1 TABLESPOON CHOPPED FRESH PARSLEY OR 1 TEASPOON DRIED PARSLEY

1 TABLESPOON VERY FINELY CHOPPED DRIED ONION

1 TABLESPOON DRIED WHOLE MARJORAM

1 LARGE BAY LEAF, CRUMBLED FINELY

¼ TEASPOON GROUND GINGER

1 TEASPOON SALT

2 TABLESPOONS RED OR WHITE WINE VINEGAR

50 g (2 oz) BROWN SUGAR

150 ml (¼ PINT) DRY WHITE OR RED WINE

150 ml (¼ PINT) STOCK MADE FROM CHICKEN STOCK CUBES

To butterfly the leg of lamb, cut down the length of the inside of the leg, carefully trim the flesh from the bone and remove the bone. Then open out the leg meat and, if necessary, slash the thicker areas to help the meat lie flat.

Combine all the remaining ingredients in a pan and heat gently for 20 minutes, stirring the sauce occasionally. Brush the sauce all over the meat.

Preheat and prepare the barbecue for grilling, following the instructions on page 30.

Place the meat on the grill, with the uncut surface (the fat side) uppermost. Cook, over medium heat, for about 40–50 minutes, or until cooked to your taste, basting it frequently with the sauce and turning it occasionally. When cooked, the butterflied leg of lamb should have a scrumptious, somewhat crusty looking, surface.

To serve, slice the lamb thinly across the grain.

Sweet and sour shoulder of lamb

SERVES 6

2 TABLESPOONS RED WINE VINEGAR

1 TABLESPOON SOY SAUCE

2 TABLESPOONS APPLE OR ORANGE JUICE

1 TABLESPOON TOMATO PURÉE

1 TABLESPOON MIRIN OR DRY SHERRY

1 GARLIC CLOVE, CHOPPED VERY FINELY

A PINCH OF GROUND GINGER

1.75–2.25 kg (4–5 lb) SHOULDER OF LAMB

SALT AND FRESHLY GROUND BLACK PEPPER

Combine the vinegar, soy sauce, fruit juice, tomato purée, mirin or sherry, garlic and ground ginger and put to one side.

Preheat and prepare the barbecue for indirect heat cooking, following the instructions on page 33.

Season the shoulder of lamb with salt and pepper. Place the shoulder, fat side up, on the grill. Cook, with medium heat, for about 1½ hours. (The exact time will depend on the shoulder weight and the required degree of cooking.) 30 minutes before the end of cooking, brush the shoulder generously with the prepared sweet and sour glaze.

Allow the roast to rest for about 15 minutes before carving.

Crown of roast lamb

A culinary work of art and a truly regal dish fit to grace any table, a crown roast may be garnished with cutlet frills and/or glacé cherries. It is wise to order a crown from your butcher in advance, but it is not all that difficult to make up your own from two matching best ends as described.

SERVES 6

2 BEST ENDS OF NECK OF LAMB

SALT AND FRESHLY GROUND BLACK PEPPER

STUFFING

25 g (1 oz) BUTTER

1 SMALL ONION, CHOPPED FINELY

1 LARGE COOKING APPLE, PEELED, CORED AND CHOPPED FINELY

250 g (8 oz) PORK SAUSAGEMEAT

3 TABLESPOONS FRESH BREADCRUMBS, TOASTED LIGHTLY

1 TABLESPOON FINELY CHOPPED FRESH PARSLEY

40 g (1½ oz) WALNUTS, CHOPPED FINELY

½ TEASPOON DRIED THYME

With a sharp, short-bladed knife, trim the meat and fat 4 cm (1½ inches) from the end of the rib bones on each joint and season. Using a trussing needle and fine string, sew the ends of the joints together back to back so the fat is inside and the bones curve upwards and outwards.

To make the stuffing, melt the butter in a pan and cook the onion gently until soft. Add the apple and continue cooking for a few minutes. Add the sausagemeat and combine well with the onion and apple. Cook for a further 3–4 minutes. Stir in the breadcrumbs, parsley, walnuts and thyme.

Preheat and prepare the barbecue for indirect heat cooking, following the instructions on page 33.

Place the crown roast on a piece of aluminium foil slightly wider than the base of the roast. Spoon the stuffing into the cavity up to 2.5 cm (1 inch) or so below the base of the trimmed bones (to allow space for the stuffing to rise). Cover the tips of the rib bones with foil to prevent charring.

Cook the lamb on the foil with medium heat, allowing 35 minutes per 500 g (1 lb). For an unstuffed crown roast, allow 30 minutes per 500 g (1 lb).

To serve, stand the crown on a serving dish and remove the foil from each bone tip. Top the bones instead with a cutlet frill. Allow two cutlets for each person.

Spit-roasted leg of lamb with garlic and oregano

SERVES 8–10

2.25–2.75 kg (5–6 lb) LEG OF LAMB

3 GARLIC CLOVES, EACH SLICED IN FOUR

1 TEASPOON SALT

1 TEASPOON DRIED OREGANO

4 TABLESPOONS MELTED BUTTER

JUICE OF 1 LEMON

Cut the surface of the meat in 12 places with a sharp-pointed knife and insert a garlic slice into each slit. Mix together the salt and oregano and push a little of the mixture into each slit. Rub the outside of the meat with any remaining mixture.

Preheat and prepare the barbecue for spit roasting, following the instructions on page 34.

Insert the spit almost parallel to the bone and test for balance before tightening the tines (spit forks). Cook the meat over medium heat.

Mix together the melted butter and lemon juice and baste the meat twice during the cooking period. If, like me, you prefer your meat done *à la Française* (slightly pink in the centre) cook it for about 1¼–1½ hours, or until the temperature reading on a meat thermometer is 60–65°C/140–150°F.

Lamb's kidney brochettes with sauce Bercy

Pictured on page 69
To add a little *je ne sais quoi* to this recipe, or indeed any other skewered lamb meat or offal dish, replace the metal skewers with sharpened branches from a mature rosemary bush. Leaving some leaves at the unsharpened end will not only help to provide a pleasant aroma during cooking, but will also prettify an otherwise plain offering.

SERVES 4

12 LAMB'S KIDNEYS

3 TABLESPOONS MELTED BUTTER

SAUCE BERCY

75 g (3 oz) BUTTER

1 TABLESPOON VERY FINELY CHOPPED SHALLOTS

300 ml (½ PINT) DRY WHITE WINE

2 TEASPOONS PLAIN FLOUR

1 TABLESPOON VERY FINELY CHOPPED FRESH PARSLEY

SALT AND FRESHLY GROUND BLACK PEPPER

Remove the fat and fine skin from the kidneys. Split each one from the inside edge to within 1 cm (½ inch) of the outer surface. Remove the white core from the inside. Thread the opened-out kidneys on to fine skewers using a wide 'stitch' across the back to hold them open.

Preheat and prepare the barbecue for grilling, following the instructions on page 30.

Prepare the sauce. Melt 25 g (1 oz) of the butter in a saucepan, add the shallots and cook until soft. Add the wine and simmer until the liquid has reduced by half. Mix the remaining butter and the flour to a paste and add a little at a time to the wine mixture.

Cook, stirring, until the mixture thickens. Stir in the parsley and add salt and pepper to taste. Keep warm while cooking the kidneys.

Brush the kidneys with half the melted butter and grill, over medium to high heat, for about 3 minutes each side, basting occasionally with the remaining butter. Do not overcook them as kidneys rapidly become tough.

Serve the kidneys with the sauce.

Herb-stuffed lamb's kidneys

SERVES 4

12 LAMB'S KIDNEYS

12 RASHERS OF PRIME STREAKY BACON

40 g (1½ oz) BUTTER, MELTED

HERB STUFFING

75 g (3 oz) FRESH WHITE BREADCRUMBS

3 TABLESPOONS CHOPPED FRESH MIXED HERBS (INCLUDING PARSLEY)

25 g (1 oz) BUTTER

1 MEDIUM-SIZE ONION, CHOPPED

1 LARGE EGG, BEATEN

SALT AND FRESHLY GROUND BLACK PEPPER

GARNISH

FRESH WATERCRESS

Skin the kidneys. Partially slit each one lengthways and remove the core. Remove the rind from the bacon rashers and spread them out on the work surface.

To make the stuffing, mix the breadcrumbs and herbs together. Melt the butter in a pan and cook the onion until soft. Stir the onion mixture into the breadcrumbs and add enough beaten egg to bind the mixture. Season well with salt and pepper.

Preheat and prepare the barbecue for grilling, following the instructions on page 30.

Spoon the prepared stuffing into the kidneys, place them at one end of the bacon rashers and roll up to enclose the kidneys.

Thread the wrapped kidneys on to skewers and brush well with the melted butter. Grill, over medium to high heat, for about 8–10 minutes or until the bacon starts to crisp. Do not overcook otherwise the kidneys will be tough and chewy.

Serve garnished with watercress.

Caul-wrapped marinated lamb's liver

Caul, a lace-like membrane of pork or lamb's fat, can be obtained from most butchers. For culinary purposes it is used to provide some protection, to offal in particular, from oven or grill heat and as a natural fat baster. Some butchers will require a day or so's notice beforehand.

SERVES 4–6

FRESH OR DRY-SALTED CAUL, PREFERABLY PORK

500–750 g (1-1½ lb) LAMB'S LIVER, IN ONE PIECE

MARINADE

2 TEASPOONS PAPRIKA

½ TEASPOON CUMIN

A PINCH OF CAYENNE PEPPER

1 TEASPOON SALT

2 TABLESPOONS LEMON JUICE

3 TABLESPOONS OLIVE OIL

TO SERVE

RED WINE VINEGAR

FRESHLY GROUND BLACK PEPPER

If the caul is dry-salted, soak it in cold water for about 20 minutes to soften it. Remove it from the water and pat dry before use.

Combine the marinade ingredients in a large bowl and mix well.

Peel away the outer membrane from the liver and cut away any coarse tubes or fibrous connective tissue. Add the liver to the marinade and leave for about 30 minutes in a cool place.

Preheat and prepare the barbecue for grilling, following the instructions on page 30.

Remove the liver and reserve the marinade. Drain the liver and wrap it in the sheet of caul until it is completely enclosed. Cook the wrapped liver, with medium heat, for 10 minutes each side until nicely browned. Baste occasionally with the reserved marinade during cooking. The liver should be cooked when it feels firm when pressed lightly.

Leave to rest in a warm place for about 10 minutes before carving. (If the barbecue has twin burners and is not being put to further use, the liver can be placed on the unlit side and the lid closed. If the day is windy and chilly, the opposite burner can be left on the lowest possible heat setting.)

Carve the caul-wrapped liver into thick slices (the heart of the liver should be pink and juicy). Provide your guests with some red wine vinegar and freshly ground black pepper for sprinkling over the liver. Serve with a salad.

Pork

Pork and apple burgers

The flavours of pork and apple combine well to make one of my favourite burgers.

SERVES 6

1 kg (2 lb) MINCED LEAN PORK

1 MEDIUM-SIZE APPLE, CHOPPED FINELY

1 EGG, BEATEN

75 g (3 oz) FRESH BREADCRUMBS

¼ TEASPOON GARLIC SALT

¼ TEASPOON ONION SALT

¼ TEASPOON FRESHLY GROUND BLACK PEPPER

2 TABLESPOONS OIL

6 HAMBURGER ROLLS, HALVED

Preheat and prepare the barbecue for grilling, following the instructions on page 30.

Mix together the pork, apple, egg and enough of the breadcrumbs to give a firm, not too wet, mixture. Carefully shape into 6 burgers.

Blend together the garlic salt, onion salt, pepper and oil and brush some of the mixture on one side of the burgers.

Grill the oiled surfaces of the burgers, over medium to high heat, for about 10 minutes. Brush the burgers with the rest of the oil mixture, turn and cook the other sides for a further 10 minutes or until nicely browned.

Toast the rolls during the last few minutes of cooking. Serve the burgers in the prepared rolls with your favourite barbecue sauce (pages 131–2).

Pork and apricot kebabs

Pictured on page 71

SERVES 4

500 g (1 lb) PORK TENDERLOIN OR BONELESS PORK LOIN

8 SHALLOTS OR 2 MEDIUM-SIZE ONIONS

250 g (8 oz) CAN OF APRICOT HALVES

175 g (6 oz) SOFT BROWN SUGAR

4 TABLESPOONS APRICOT JAM

6 TABLESPOONS RED OR WHITE WINE VINEGAR

3 TABLESPOONS SOY SAUCE

1 TEASPOON MUSTARD POWDER

SALT AND FRESHLY GROUND BLACK PEPPER

Preheat and prepare the barbecue for grilling, following the instructions on page 30.

Cut the pork into 2.5 cm (1-inch) cubes.

If using shallots, parboil them for about 5 minutes; if using onions, parboil them whole for about 6–7 minutes and then cut into quarters. Drain the apricot halves, reserving the juice.

Thread the pork cubes, shallots or onion quarters and apricot halves on to skewers.

Combine the remaining ingredients in a small saucepan and heat gently until the sugar has dissolved. Brush the kebabs all over with the mixture. Place them on the grill and cook, over medium heat, for about 15 minutes. Turn and baste the kebabs several times during cooking.

Note: pineapple chunks may be used instead of the apricot halves. In which case, replace the apricot jam with marmalade and half the wine vinegar with the same quantity of pineapple juice.

Turkistan kebabs

Page 60

Lamb's kidney brochettes with sauce Bercy

Page 66

*Butterflied
leg of lamb in a
herb crust*

Page 64

*Soy-glazed
roast loin
of pork*
Page 79

*Garlic
and gingered
spare ribs*
Page 76

*Pork
and apricot
kebabs*
Page 68

Stir-fried pork
with oyster sauce
Page 75

Indonesian pork satay with peanut sauce

SERVES 6

1.1 kg (2½ lb) BONELESS PORK LOIN

3 TABLESPOONS SOY SAUCE

3 TABLESPOONS GROUNDNUT OIL, PLUS EXTRA FOR BASTING

1 TABLESPOON CHOPPED ONION

1 GARLIC CLOVE, CRUSHED

1 TEASPOON SUGAR

A PINCH OF MILD CURRY POWDER

PEANUT SAUCE

50 g (2 oz) SHREDDED COCONUT FLESH

150 ml (¼ PINT) HOT MILK

2 TABLESPOONS SOFT BUTTER

½ TEASPOON MILD CURRY POWDER

½ TEASPOON FRESHLY GRATED ROOT GINGER

1 GARLIC CLOVE, CHOPPED VERY FINELY

1 MEDIUM-SIZE ONION, CHOPPED FINELY

50 g (2 oz) CRUSHED PINEAPPLE

150 ml (¼ PINT) CHICKEN STOCK

2 TABLESPOONS SUGAR

3 TABLESPOONS CRUNCHY PEANUT BUTTER

½ TEASPOON SALT

A PINCH OF FRESHLY GROUND BLACK PEPPER

Cut the pork into 2.5 × 10 × 5 mm (1- × 4- × ¼-inch) strips. Soak some skewers in water if using bamboo.

Combine the soy sauce, oil, onion, garlic, sugar and curry powder. Marinate the meat strips in the mixture, in the refrigerator, for 2–3 hours, stirring occasionally.

Meanwhile, make the sauce. Soak the shredded coconut in the milk for about 30 minutes. Then melt the butter in an ovenproof dish or deep frying pan, add the curry powder and cook, over fairly gentle heat, for 1 minute. Add the ginger, garlic and onion and continue to cook for 5 minutes. Add the soaked coconut and milk, pineapple, chicken stock, sugar and peanut butter. Season to taste with the salt and

pepper and cook for 15–20 minutes, stirring occasionally.

Preheat and prepare the barbecue for grilling, following the instructions on page 30.

Drain the meat and thread on to thin metal skewers or soaked bamboo sticks. Cook, over medium to high heat, for 5–10 minutes. Turn and baste frequently with groundnut oil.

Serve the meat with the peanut sauce.

Sweet and sour pork

Pictured on the front cover

SERVES 4

250 g (8 oz) LEAN PORK

1 TEASPOON SOY SAUCE

1 TEASPOON RICE WINE OR DRY SHERRY

1 TEASPOON FINELY GRATED FRESH ROOT GINGER

2 DRIED MUSHROOMS OR 2 OPEN-CUP MUSHROOMS

½ MEDIUM-SIZE ONION

1 MEDIUM-SIZE GREEN PEPPER

25 g (1 oz) CANNED BAMBOO SHOOTS

50 g (2 oz) CARROT

900 ml (1½ PINTS) OIL FOR DEEP-FRYING

1½ TABLESPOONS CORNFLOUR

2 TABLESPOONS VEGETABLE OIL

1 GARLIC CLOVE, CHOPPED FINELY

SALT

SAUCE

6 TABLESPOONS CHICKEN STOCK

1½ TABLESPOONS SOY SAUCE

5 TABLESPOONS SUGAR

1 TABLESPOON TOMATO KETCHUP

½ TEASPOON SALT

1 TABLESPOON CORNFLOUR, DISSOLVED IN 2 TABLESPOONS WATER

4 TABLESPOONS RED OR WHITE WINE VINEGAR

2 SLICES OF CANNED PINEAPPLE, CUT INTO 6 PIECES

Cut the pork into bite-size cubes and combine with the soy sauce, rice wine or sherry and grated ginger. Leave to marinate for about 15 minutes.

If using dried mushrooms, soak them in warm water until soft; then remove. Discard the stalks of the dried or fresh mushrooms and cut the caps into thin slices.

Preheat and prepare the barbecue for wok-cooking, following the instructions on page 38.

Slice the onion into bite-size pieces. De-seed the pepper and cut it into bite-size pieces. Cut the bamboo shoots into thin slices. Slice the carrot into thin rounds and parboil in lightly salted water. Rinse with cold water and drain.

Add the oil for deep-frying to the wok. Position the wok on the barbecue and heat the oil, over high heat, to 180°C/350°F. Add the cornflour to the pork cubes and turn them until evenly coated. Deep-fry the cubes until they are golden brown; then remove from the wok and drain.

Pour off the oil from the wok and replace with the vegetable oil. Heat the oil and quickly stir-fry the garlic. Add the mushrooms, onion, bamboo shoots, pepper and carrot, stir-frying very briefly between each addition.

Mix together the chicken stock, soy sauce, sugar, ketchup and salt and add this to the vegetables. Bring the sauce rapidly to the boil and then quickly mix in the dissolved cornflour, stirring constantly. When the sauce has thickened, add the pork cubes and vinegar; then add the pineapple pieces and stir well. Serve immediately.

Stir-fried pork with mushrooms and cabbage

Stir-frying can be likened to a dance – slow, quick, quick, slow. The first step in the dance is the patient preparation that needs to be carried out *before* heating the wok. This involves slicing, chopping, mixing and, perhaps, marinating the food (individual ingredients, when prepared, can be packed in plastic bags or covered bowls and kept in the refrigerator until required). Stir-frying the prepared food constitutes the quick-steps. This high speed action demands that the prepared food, cooking implements and serving dishes are easily to hand. The final slow step is when you and your 'partners' sit down to savour and enjoy the food.

SERVES 4

750 g (1½ lb) LEAN PORK, SLICED THINLY

¼ TEASPOON SALT

1 TABLESPOON CORNFLOUR

3 TABLESPOONS VEGETABLE OIL

500 g (1 lb) SPRING CABBAGE

3 TABLESPOONS LARD

250 g (8 oz) OPEN-CUP MUSHROOMS, HALVED OR SLICED AND STALKS DISCARDED

1½ TABLESPOONS SOY SAUCE

3 TABLESPOONS CHICKEN STOCK

½ TEASPOON SESAME OIL

2 TEASPOONS SUGAR

Preheat and prepare the barbecue for wok-cooking, following the instructions on page 38.

Cut the pork into thin bite-size slices. Sprinkle with the salt, cornflour and 1 tablespoon of the vegetable oil and mix together lightly.

Remove the tougher stems from the cabbage and cut the leaves into 5 cm (2-inch) pieces.

Position the wok on the barbecue and melt the lard. When hot, add the mushrooms and cabbage. Stir-fry over high heat for 1½ minutes. Add the soy sauce and chicken stock and continue to stir-fry for 1 minute. Place the lid over the wok (or bring down the lid of the barbecue if you do not have a wok lid) and cook, over medium heat, for a further 2 minutes. Turn out the vegetables on to a warmed dish and cover.

Pour the remaining vegetable oil into the wok and, when hot, add the pork and stir-fry, over high heat, for 2½–3 minutes. Add the sesame oil and sugar and stir-fry for a further 2 minutes. Return the vegetables to the pork and stir and mix together for 1 minute.

Serve immediately, with rice or noodles.

Stir-fried pork with oyster sauce

Pictured on page 72

SERVES 4

250 g (8 oz) LEAN PORK, PREFERABLY TENDERLOIN

250 g (8 oz) SPINACH

3 TABLESPOONS VEGETABLE OIL

½ TEASPOON SALT

¼ TEASPOON SUGAR

1 TABLESPOON WATER

2 TABLESPOONS OYSTER SAUCE

6 BABY SWEETCORN, BROKEN INTO PIECES

½ TEASPOON SESAME OIL

FRESHLY GROUND BLACK PEPPER

MARINADE

¼ TEASPOON SOY SAUCE

½ TEASPOON SESAME OIL

½ TEASPOON RICE WINE OR DRY SHERRY

½ TEASPOON SUGAR

1 EGG YOLK

1 TABLESPOON CORNFLOUR

SALT AND FRESHLY GROUND BLACK PEPPER

Preheat and prepare the barbecue for wok-cooking, following the instructions on page 38.

Slice the pork into bite-size pieces.

For the marinade, combine the soy sauce, sesame oil, rice wine or sherry, sugar, egg yolk and salt and pepper to taste and mix well. Stir the pork into this mixture and marinate for about 10 minutes. Stir in the cornflour just before cooking.

Cut the spinach into 5 cm (2-inch) lengths. Position the wok on the barbecue and heat 1 tablespoon of the vegetable oil. Add the salt and the spinach and stir-fry quickly over high heat. Add the sugar and water and stir again. Drain the liquid from the wok, remove the spinach and keep warm.

Heat the remaining vegetable oil in the wok and stir-fry the pork until golden brown all over. Remove the pork from the wok and keep warm.

Add the oyster sauce to the wok and when the liquid begins to bubble, return the pork pieces to it and stir-fry for about a minute. Return the spinach and add the baby sweetcorn pieces. Sprinkle with the sesame oil and black pepper to taste and stir for another minute or so.

Serve immediately.

Spiced orange spare ribs

Orange juice, lemon juice, Worcestershire sauce and honey combine to give the ribs a delicious spicy flavour and a handsome glaze.

SERVES 4

1.25 kg (3 lb) LEAN SPARE RIBS

MARINADE

2 TABLESPOONS CLEAR HONEY

JUICE OF ½ LEMON

GRATED ZEST OF ½ AND JUICE OF 2 ORANGES

2 TABLESPOONS WORCESTERSHIRE SAUCE

2 TEASPOONS SOY SAUCE

SALT

Mix together the marinade ingredients in a pan and heat gently. Simmer for 2 minutes and allow to cool.

If the ribs are in whole slabs, cut into sections of three or four ribs. Place the ribs, together with the marinade, in a plastic bag and securely close the bag with a twist-tie. Put the bag in a roasting pan or similar dish (in case of leakage) and refrigerate for 12–24 hours, turning over the bag occasionally.

Preheat and prepare the barbecue for grilling, following the instructions on page 30.

Briefly drain the spare ribs and reserve the marinade. Cook the ribs, over medium heat, for about 1¼ hours* or until the meat has pulled away from the rib ends exposing 1–2 cm (½–¾ inch) of bone. Turn the ribs frequently during the cooking time, but baste occasionally only during the final 15 minutes so the surface of the ribs doesn't become charred. When properly cooked the spare ribs will have a deep golden, semi-translucent appearance and the meat will be tender and juicy.

* If the ribs are 'mean on meat', the cooking time given can be reduced considerably.

Garlic and gingered spare ribs

Pictured on page 71

SERVES 6–8

2.75 kg (6 lb) LEAN SPARE RIBS

MARINADE

4 GARLIC CLOVES, CHOPPED VERY FINELY

2 TABLESPOONS PRESERVED GINGER, CHOPPED FINELY

275 ml (9 fl oz) CHICKEN STOCK

125 g (4 oz) ORANGE MARMALADE

3 TABLESPOONS RED WINE VINEGAR

3 TABLESPOONS TOMATO KETCHUP

2 TEASPOONS SOY SAUCE

Mix together the garlic, ginger, stock, marmalade, vinegar, ketchup and soy sauce to make a marinade.

Place a large plastic bag in a roasting pan or large dish. If the ribs are in whole slabs, cut them into sections of three or four ribs. Put the ribs in the bag and pour in the marinade. Securely close the bag with a twist-tie. Place the tin or dish in the refrigerator and leave for 12–24 hours, turning the bag over occasionally.

Preheat and prepare the barbecue for grilling, following the instructions on page 30.

Remove the ribs from the marinade and drain briefly, reserving the marinade. Cook, over medium heat, for about 1¼ hours or until the meat pulls away from the end of the rib bones. Turn the ribs frequently but baste only occasionally, and not too liberally, with the reserved marinade.

Lemony pork chops

SERVES 4

4 LOIN OR CHUMP CHOPS, CUT 2.5 cm (1 INCH) THICK

MARINADE

JUICE AND GRATED ZEST OF 1 LEMON

4 BAY LEAVES

4 TABLESPOONS OIL

1 TABLESPOON CHOPPED FRESH PARSLEY

A PINCH OF DRIED OREGANO

A PINCH OF DRIED THYME

A PINCH OF DRIED SAGE

A PINCH OF SALT

¼ TEASPOON FRESHLY GROUND BLACK PEPPER

1 GARLIC CLOVE, CRUSHED

Wipe the chops and slash the fat around the edge of each at 1 cm (½-inch) intervals.

Combine the marinade ingredients. Place the chops in a shallow dish and spoon the marinade over the meat. Cover the dish and refrigerate for 6–24 hours, turning the chops over once or twice.

Preheat and prepare the barbecue for grilling, following the instructions on page 30.

Reserving the marinade, remove the chops and place on the grill. Cook, over medium to high heat, for 15–20 minutes each side or until all the pink colour in the centre of the meat has disappeared. Baste the chops occasionally with the marinade during cooking.

Spicy pork chops

The delicious spicy flavour comes from a combination of Dijon mustard, soy sauce, chilli powder and honey.

SERVES 6

6 PORK LOIN CHOPS, 2.5 cm (1 INCH) THICK

6 TABLESPOONS CLEAR HONEY

6 TABLESPOONS DIJON MUSTARD

2 TABLESPOONS SOY SAUCE

¼ TEASPOON CHILLI POWDER

¼ TEASPOON SALT

Wipe the chops and slash the fat around the edge of each at 1 cm (½-inch) intervals.

Mix together the honey, mustard, soy sauce, chilli powder and salt.

Place the chops in a shallow dish and spoon the marinade over the meat. Cover the dish and refrigerate for 6–24 hours, turning the chops over once or twice.

Preheat and prepare the barbecue for grilling, following the instructions on page 30.

Reserving the marinade, remove the chops and place on the grill. Cook, over medium to high heat, for 15–20 minutes each side or until all the pink colour in the centre of the meat has disappeared. Baste the chops with the marinade just before turning and during the final few minutes of cooking.

Grilled gammon steaks with spicy apple sauce

SERVES 4

3 TABLESPOONS APPLE SAUCE

2 TABLESPOONS ORANGE JUICE

1 TEASPOON GRATED ORANGE ZEST

2 TEASPOONS DIJON MUSTARD

A PINCH OF DRIED THYME

A PINCH OF DRIED SAGE

4 GAMMON STEAKS

Preheat and prepare the barbecue for grilling, following the instructions on page 30.

Mix together the apple sauce, orange juice and zest, and stir in the mustard, thyme and sage.

Brush the apple mixture over one side of the gammon steaks. Grill the coated side, over medium heat, for about 3 minutes. Brush the top of the steaks with more mixture, turn over and grill for a further 3 minutes. Continue brushing and turning the steaks until done.

Serve immediately, with some additional apple sauce and mustard.

Oriental pork belly

Oriental Pork Belly tastes delicious hot or cold and goes well with jacket potatoes.

SERVES 6–8

1.25 kg (3 lb) BELLY OF PORK ON THE BONE

MARINADE

1 GARLIC CLOVE

½ TEASPOON SALT

3 TABLESPOONS SOY SAUCE

4 TABLESPOONS CLEAR HONEY

½ TEASPOON GROUND CINNAMON

Using a sharp knife, carefully remove the rind from the pork leaving the fat intact.

Score the fat in a diamond pattern.

Crush the garlic clove and salt together in a pestle and mortar (or use a spoon and a saucer). Mix the garlic, soy sauce, honey and cinnamon in a shallow dish.

Place the pork, skin side down, in the marinade. Cover the dish and refrigerate for 6–24 hours. Remove the dish from the refrigerator an hour or so before the meat is cooked.

Preheat and prepare the barbecue for indirect heat cooking, following the instructions on page 33. Half-fill a roasting tin with hot water and cover with a wire rack. Place the roasting tin on the unlit side of the barbecue.

Remove the meat from the marinade, reserving the marinade. Place the meat in the centre of the wire rack.

Cook, with medium heat, for 1 hour. Turn the meat over and baste with the remaining marinade. Cook the meat for a further 1 hour.

Allow the meat to stand for 10 minutes. Cut the pork into thin slices down to the bone.

Baked ham with brown sugar glaze

2.25 kg (5 lb) PIECE OF MIDDLE CUT GAMMON, ROLLED

750 ml (1¼ PINTS) DRY CIDER

1 MEDIUM-SIZE ONION, STUCK WITH 6–10 CLOVES

2 BAY LEAVES

6 BLACK PEPPERCORNS

ABOUT 36 CLOVES

BROWN SUGAR GLAZE

125 g (4 oz) BROWN SUGAR

½ TEASPOON GROUND CINNAMON

1 TABLESPOON ENGLISH MUSTARD

4 TABLESPOONS BEER, CIDER OR CRANBERRY, APPLE OR ORANGE JUICE

Soak the gammon in cold water for a few hours (change the water during this period). Remove the joint and place in a saucepan or casserole that will accommodate it comfortably.

Pour over 600 ml (1 pint) of the cider plus enough cold water to cover the gammon completely. Add the onion, bay leaves and peppercorns. Bring to the boil and simmer gently for 1 hour.

Drain the gammon, let it cool a little, remove the string and carefully cut off the skin. Stand the gammon, fat side uppermost, in a roasting tin. Pour the remainder of the cider into the tin. Lightly score the fat in diagonal lines (about 2.5 cm, 1 inch apart) in different directions to form diamond shapes.

Preheat and prepare the barbecue for indirect heat cooking, following the instructions on page 33.

Combine the sugar, cinnamon, mustard and beer, cider or fruit juice in a small saucepan and heat gently until the sugar has dissolved. Brush the glaze mixture all over the joint. Insert a clove in the centre of each diamond shape.

Bake the gammon, with medium heat, for 1–1¼ hours, basting occasionally with the cider-enriched juices.

Roast loin of pork with ambrosia stuffing

SERVES 6–8

1.75 kg (4 lb) LOIN OF PORK, BONED AND ROLLED

AMBROSIA STUFFING

3 TABLESPOONS SOFT BUTTER, PLUS 3 TABLESPOONS MELTED BUTTER

2 MEDIUM-SIZE ONIONS, CHOPPED

2 MEDIUM-SIZE COOKING OR EATING APPLES, CORED, PEELED AND CHOPPED

175 g (6 oz) RIPE OLIVES, STONED AND CHOPPED

75 g (3 oz) WALNUTS, CHOPPED

¼ TEASPOON DRIED THYME

½ TEASPOON SALT

75 g (3 oz) FRESH BREADCRUMBS

75 g (3 oz) COOKED HAM, CHOPPED

Preheat and prepare the barbecue for indirect heat cooking, following the instructions on page 33.

Using a sharp knife, slice the loin halfway down at 2.5 cm (1-inch) intervals. Then cut down further into each incision to form deep pockets, taking care to leave a 2.5 cm (1-inch) wall on the sides and bottom of the loin roll.

To make the stuffing, heat the soft butter in a skillet or pan and cook the onions, stirring occasionally, until transparent. Add the apples and continue cooking for 1 minute. Add the olives, walnuts, thyme, salt, breadcrumbs, melted butter and ham and mix well.

Fill each pocket in the meat generously with the stuffing. Tie the roll lengthways at 2.5 cm (1-inch) intervals to hold it firmly together.

Roast, with medium to high heat, for about 1½–2 hours until the meat is well done. (A meat thermometer buried in the centre of the roast should register 85°C/185°F.)

Remove the roast from the barbecue and allow to stand for about 10 minutes before carving. Remove the string and slice through the meat between the pockets to make individually stuffed portions.

Soy-glazed roast loin of pork

Pictured on page 71

The combination of soy sauce, apple juice, garlic and ginger on the skin of the loin produces a very dark and handsome glaze. For those who like the crisp, tasty crackling, serve the meat with a strip or two and an extra serviette. This dish is equally delicious served hot or cold.

SERVES 6–8

125 ml (4 fl oz) APPLE JUICE

3 TABLESPOONS SOY SAUCE

1 GARLIC CLOVE, CHOPPED VERY FINELY

1 TEASPOON FRESHLY GRATED ROOT GINGER OR ¼ TEASPOON GROUND GINGER

1.75 kg (4 lb) LOIN OF PORK

Preheat and prepare the barbecue for indirect heat cooking, following the instructions on page 33 (use a drip pan).

Mix together the apple juice, soy sauce, garlic and ginger and place on one side.

With a sharp, short-bladed knife score the skin of the loin at roughly 1 cm (½-inch) intervals.

Roast the loin, fat side up, with medium heat for 1 hour. Generously baste the scored skin with the marinade. Cook the meat for a further 1½ hours or until the meat is well done (a meat thermometer inserted into the thickest part should register 85°C/185°F). Baste frequently during the final 30 minutes of cooking to produce an attractive dark glaze.

Use the juices collected in the drip pan to make a rich gravy.

Poultry & game

Chicken satay with Indonesian sauce

SERVES 4

INGREDIENTS FOR 1 QUANTITY OF INDONESIAN SAUCE (PAGE 132)

750 g (1½ lb) CHICKEN BREASTS, BONED AND SKINNED

GROUNDNUT OIL FOR BRUSHING

MARINADE

1 GARLIC CLOVE, CRUSHED

2 TABLESPOONS SOY SAUCE

JUICE OF 1 LEMON

TO SERVE

SHREDDED LETTUCE

Prepare the Indonesian Sauce 2 or 3 hours before cooking the chicken, following the instructions on page 132. Soak some skewers in water if using bamboo.

Cut the meat into 2.5 cm (1-inch) cubes. Mix together the marinade ingredients in a bowl and add the chicken cubes, turning to coat with the mixture. Cover the bowl and leave to marinate for about 30 minutes.

Preheat and prepare the barbecue for grilling, following the instructions on page 30.

Remove the meat from the marinade and thread them on to soaked bamboo or metal skewers. Reheat the sauce gently, adding a little water if it is too thick. Brush the meat with a little oil and grill, over medium heat, for about 6–8 minutes or until the meat is cooked.

Serve the chicken on a dish lined with shredded lettuce and accompanied by the Indonesian Sauce.

Chicken suprême au avocat

Another one of those recipes more in keeping with semi-formal intimate parties – it should inspire at least five minutes worth of 'foody' chit-chat.

SERVES 4

2 WHOLE CHICKEN BREASTS, SKINNED

150 ml (¼ PINT) DRY WHITE WINE

75 ml (3 fl oz) OIL

2 GARLIC CLOVES, CRUSHED

½ TEASPOON SALT

2 RIPE MEDIUM-SIZE AVOCADOS

JUICE OF 1 LEMON

2 SMALL EGGS (SIZE 4), HARD-BOILED

SAUCE

150 ml (¼ PINT) MAYONNAISE

2 TABLESPOONS CLEAR HONEY

1 TABLESPOON DIJON MUSTARD

75 ml (3 fl oz) OIL

4 TABLESPOONS FINELY CHOPPED ONION

1 TEASPOON VERY FINELY CHOPPED FRESH PARSLEY

JUICE OF ½ LEMON

Place the breasts on a board, cut sides up, and cover with two sheets of greaseproof paper. Using a rolling pin or the flat surface of a meat hammer, beat out the breasts thinly (roughly doubling the area).

Combine the wine, oil, garlic and salt in a shallow dish. Place the flattened breasts in the mixture, turning them over twice to coat fully, and leave to marinate for 30–40 minutes. Soak some wooden cocktail sticks.

To make the sauce, mix together the mayonnaise, honey, mustard, oil, onion, parsley and lemon juice and put to one side.

Preheat and prepare the barbecue for indirect heat cooking, following the instructions on page 33.

Cut each avocado in half lengthways, remove the stone and carefully remove the tough outer skin. Coat the flesh with the lemon juice to stop it going brown. Place a hard-boiled egg in the recess left by the stone and cover with the other half of the avocado.

Drain the chicken breasts (reserving the marinade), pat them dry and wrap each around a re-assembled avocado. Secure the edges with the soaked wooden cocktail sticks.

Cook the chicken packages, with medium heat, for about 30 minutes. Turn the packages occasionally during cooking, basting them generously each time with the reserved marinade. When fully cooked the meat will be firm and springy to the touch.

Let the stuffed breasts stand for about 10 minutes before serving. Cut each one in half lengthways, spoon a little of the sauce over the portions and serve the remainder separately.

Honsoywin chicken quarters

A very tasty dish to set before your guests, but take care not to over-baste as this could make the skin too dark or burnt. Aim for a deep golden 'mahogany' colour with a nicely lacquered overcoat.

SERVES 4

4 CHICKEN QUARTERS

MARINADE

4 TABLESPOONS CLEAR HONEY

4 TABLESPOONS SOY SAUCE

150 ml (¼ PINT) WHITE WINE

150 ml (¼ PINT) ORANGE JUICE

¼ TEASPOON GROUND ALLSPICE

1 TEASPOON PAPRIKA

1 GARLIC CLOVE, CRUSHED

2 TABLESPOONS WATER

Place the chicken quarters in a dish.

To make the marinade, mix together all the ingredients. Pour the marinade over the chicken quarters, turning them to ensure an even coating. Cover the dish and leave in the refrigerator for a few hours or overnight; turn the pieces occasionally during this time.

Preheat and prepare the barbecue for grilling, following the instructions on page 30.

Drain the chicken pieces, reserving the marinade, and place on the grill. Cook, over medium heat, for 40–50 minutes or until both sides are fully cooked, basting with the marinade several times. To check if each quarter is cooked, pierce the thickest part with a skewer – the juices should run clear. If in any doubt, cut the meat to the bone, in this thick part, and look to see that the meat next to the bone is no longer pink.

Chicken with chilli glaze

Pictured on the front cover
Your primary aim as a barbecue cook is to create maximum visual appeal in order to get everyone's taste buds stimulated well before they get their teeth into the food. This colourful, red-glazed chicken does just that and tastes good too!

SERVES 4

4 TABLESPOONS MELTED BUTTER

1 TEASPOON CHILLI POWDER

2 GARLIC CLOVES, CHOPPED VERY FINELY

2 TABLESPOONS LIME JUICE

½ TEASPOON GRATED LIME ZEST

¼ TEASPOON GROUND CUMIN

1.25 kg (3 lb) CHICKEN, JOINTED

Preheat and prepare the barbecue for grilling, following the instructions on page 30.

Mix together the butter, chilli powder, garlic, lime juice and zest and cumin. Generously brush the chicken pieces with the mixture.

Place the chicken pieces, skin side up, on the grill and grill over medium to high heat for about 40 minutes, turning the pieces and basting frequently, until the meat is cooked.

Tandoori chicken

In spite of the number of spices in this recipe, the end result is fairly mild. Bottled tandoori paste is now readily available if you don't have time to make your own.

SERVES 4

3 × 1 kg (2 lb) FRESH CHICKENS

JUICE OF 1½ LEMONS

MELTED GHEE OR VEGETABLE OIL FOR BRUSHING

TANDOORI MARINADE

4 MEDIUM-SIZE GARLIC CLOVES

1 cm (½-INCH) PIECE OF FRESH ROOT GINGER, PEELED AND CHOPPED

1 TEASPOON GROUND ROASTED CUMIN SEEDS

½ TEASPOON GROUND CARDAMOM

½ TEASPOON GROUND CINNAMON

¼ TEASPOON GROUND NUTMEG

½ TEASPOON CHILI POWDER

½ TEASPOON CAYENNE PEPPER

1 TEASPOON SALT

125 ml (4 fl oz) NATURAL YOGURT

Cut the chickens into quarters and remove the wings from the breast pieces. Pull the skin from all the quarters (kitchen paper will help provide a better grip); then pierce the flesh all over with the point of a skewer or a sharp-pointed kitchen fork. Make deep diagonal slashes in the meat about 2.5 cm (1 inch) apart.

Place the portions in a large bowl. Sprinkle over the lemon juice and rub in well for a minute or two. Cover the bowl and leave for 30 minutes.

For the tandoori marinade, put all the ingredients in a food processor or blender and blend until the mixture is smooth. Pour the marinade over the chicken portions and mix thoroughly to coat well. Cover the bowl again and leave the chicken to marinate for at least 4 hours or overnight in the refrigerator. Remove the bowl from the refrigerator at least 1 hour before cooking.

Preheat and prepare the barbecue for

grilling, following the instructions on page 30.

Place the chicken portions on the grill, bone side down, and brush the slashed surface of the meat with melted ghee or oil. Cook, over medium to high heat, for about 10 minutes. Turn and baste the other side and cook for a further 10 minutes. Continue to cook, turning and basting the chicken every 10 minutes or until the meat is cooked – this will take 30–40 minutes.

Serve the chicken with lemon wedges and a salad.

Sweet and sour chicken

<u>SERVES 4</u>

1.25–1.5 kg (3–3½ lb) CHICKEN

150 ml (¼ PINT) SOY SAUCE

200 g (7 oz) CAN OF PINEAPPLE CHUNKS

150 ml (¼ PINT) CHICKEN STOCK

2 GARLIC CLOVES, CHOPPED VERY FINELY

1 TABLESPOON FRESHLY GRATED ROOT GINGER OR 1 TEASPOON GROUND GINGER

50 g (2 oz) BROWN SUGAR

3 TABLESPOONS RED OR WHITE WINE VINEGAR

1 GREEN PEPPER, DE-SEEDED AND CUT INTO 2.5 cm (1-INCH) SQUARES

1 FIRM, RIPE TOMATO, SKINNED, DE-SEEDED AND CHOPPED

4 SPRING ONIONS, SLICED DIAGONALLY INTO 2.5 cm (1-INCH) PIECES

2 TABLESPOONS CORNFLOUR

3 TABLESPOONS COLD WATER

Using a heavy kitchen cleaver, joint and cut the chicken into 5 cm (2-inch) pieces.

Combine the soy sauce, the pineapple juice from the can, the chicken stock, garlic, ginger, brown sugar and vinegar and mix well. Marinate the chicken pieces in the mixture, in a cool place, for 2–3 hours. Remove the chicken pieces from the marinade about 30 minutes before cooking. Reserve the marinade.

Preheat and prepare the barbecue for

indirect heat cooking, following the instructions on page 33.

Brown the chicken pieces for about 15 minutes over the lit side of the barbecue. Transfer the part-cooked chicken to a deep-sided roasting tin. Arrange the pepper, tomato, pineapple chunks and spring onions around the chicken pieces and pour the reserved marinade over. Position the roasting tin over the unlit side of the barbecue and cook, with low to medium heat, for about 30 minutes.

When the chicken pieces are cooked, remove them to a warm dish. Mix the cornflour and water to a paste and stir into the hot juices. Carefully move the pan over to the lit side of the barbecue and simmer gently, stirring continuously, until the sauce has thickened.

Allow your guests to pour the hot sauce over the chicken and serve it with rice and a salad.

Grilled poussins with mustard

If you can't buy poussins, very small chickens, about 375 g (12 oz) in weight, may be used instead.

<u>SERVES 4</u>

4 POUSSINS

125 ml (4 fl oz) GROUNDNUT OIL

1 TABLESPOON FRENCH MUSTARD

1 TEASPOON DRIED ROSEMARY

1 TEASPOON DRIED THYME

2 BAY LEAVES, CRUSHED

DRY WHITE BREADCRUMBS FOR SPRINKLING

SALT AND FRESHLY GROUND BLACK PEPPER

Preheat and prepare the barbecue for grilling, following the instructions on page 30.

Split the poussins in half from the back,

open them out and gently crush the bones by pressing down with a large heavy-bladed knife or cleaver so that they lie flat whilst cooking. Season the poussins.

Combine the oil, mustard, rosemary, thyme and bay leaves and mix well.

Brush some of the mixture over the poussins and grill them, bone side down, over medium to high heat, for about 10 minutes. Turn and grill the other side for 10–15 minutes or until cooked.

Brush the rest of the mustard mixture over the poussins and scatter with breadcrumbs. Return the poussins to the grill and cook for a further 2–3 minutes or until nicely browned.

Sesame gingered chicken

SERVES 4

8 CHICKEN THIGHS OR DRUMSTICKS

MARINADE

2.5 cm (1-INCH) PIECE OF FRESH ROOT GINGER, PEELED AND GRATED

2 TABLESPOONS SESAME SEEDS

2 TEASPOONS SESAME OIL

1 TABLESPOON GROUNDNUT OIL

1 GARLIC CLOVE, CHOPPED VERY FINELY

¼ TEASPOON CAYENNE PEPPER

25 g (1 oz) SPRING ONION, CHOPPED FINELY

Wash the chicken thighs or drumsticks and pat dry.

Combine the marinade ingredients and mix thoroughly. Brush the marinade all over the thighs or drumsticks and place in a dish. Cover the dish and leave in the refrigerator for a few hours or overnight.

Preheat and prepare the barbecue for grilling, following the instructions on page 30.

Lightly drain the thighs or drumsticks, reserving any marinade. Grill, over medium

to high heat, for about 30 minutes or until nicely browned and cooked, turning and basting with the marinade a few times during cooking.

Streaky drumsticks

Pictured on page 90

SERVES 4

8 PLUMP CHICKEN DRUMSTICKS

75 g (3 oz) CREAM CHEESE

8 RASHERS OF STREAKY BACON

GROUNDNUT OR SUNFLOWER OIL FOR BASTING

SALT AND FRESHLY GROUND BLACK PEPPER

Soak 8 wooden cocktail sticks in water. Preheat and prepare the barbecue for grilling, following the instructions on page 30.

Using a short, sharp knife, make a deep incision in the fattest part of each drumstick and fill the slit with cream cheese. Season; then wrap a rasher of bacon around each drumstick and secure in place with the soaked wooden cocktail sticks.

Cook, over medium to high heat, basting frequently with oil, for about 12 minutes each side or until cooked.

Teriyaki turkey drumsticks

Pictured on page 90

If unable to buy small drumsticks (it appears to be easier to purchase turkey drumsticks more akin in size to small legs of lamb), part-cook the larger drumsticks in the barbecue using the indirect heat method (page 33), or in the kitchen oven, before finishing them off on the grill.

SERVES 6

6 SMALL TURKEY DRUMSTICKS

MARINADE

150 ml (¼ PINT) SOY SAUCE

4 TABLESPOONS CLEAR HONEY

3 TABLESPOONS MIRIN OR DRY SHERRY

2 TEASPOONS FRESHLY GRATED ROOT GINGER OR ½ TEASPOON GROUND GINGER

150 ml (¼ PINT) OIL

2 GARLIC CLOVES, CRUSHED

50 g (2 oz) SPRING ONION, SLICED THINLY

Wash the drumsticks, pat dry and pierce all over with the point of a skewer.

Combine all the marinade ingredients and mix well. Pour over the drumsticks, turning them to make sure they are well coated. Cover the dish and leave in the refrigerator for a few hours or overnight. Turn the drumsticks occasionally while they are in the marinade.

Preheat and prepare the barbecue for grilling, following the instructions on page 30.

Briefly drain the drumsticks (reserve the marinade) and place on the grill. Cook the drumsticks over medium to high heat for about 40–50 minutes or until cooked, turning and basting frequently with the marinade. To check if they are cooked, pierce the thickest part with a skewer – the juices should run clear. If in doubt, cut the meat in the same area and look to see that the meat next to the bone is no longer pink.

Orange burgundy duckling

SERVES 4

1.75–2.25 kg (4–5 lb) DUCKLING

300 ml (½ PINT) BURGUNDY WINE

1 TEASPOON SALT

1 TEASPOON FRESHLY GROUND BLACK PEPPER

¼ TEASPOON DRIED THYME

1 ORANGE, QUARTERED

2 SLICES OF ONION

1 CELERY TOP

150 ml (¼ PINT) CONCENTRATED ORANGE JUICE

GARNISH

THINLY SLICED ORANGES

Preheat and prepare the barbecue for indirect heat cooking, following the instructions on page 33 (use a drip pan).

Remove any giblets from the duckling. Wash and pat dry, inside and out, with kitchen paper.

Brush the cavity of the duckling with a little of the burgundy and sprinkle with the salt, pepper and thyme. Place the orange, onion and celery inside and close the cavity with fine skewers.

Mix together the remaining burgundy and the orange juice and use it to brush the outside of the duckling.

Roast the duckling with medium to high heat for about 2 hours or until tender, pricking the thigh and breast skin with a fine, sharp-pointed skewer or large needle and basting with the wine mixture after 30 minutes. Baste frequently during cooking.

Discard the flavourings in the cavity and cut the duckling into portions. Place them on a hot serving dish. If desired, skim the fat from the pan juices and pour the juices over the portions. Arrange orange slices around the edge of the dish.

Spit-roasted glazed duckling

SERVES 3–4

1.75–2.25 kg (4–5 lb) PLUMP YOUNG DUCKLING

MARINADE

4 TABLESPOONS DRY RED WINE

1 TEASPOON SOY SAUCE

2 TABLESPOONS SUGAR

3 TABLESPOONS GROUNDNUT OIL

1 TEASPOON PAPRIKA

½ TEASPOON FRESHLY GRATED ROOT GINGER OR A GOOD PINCH OF GROUND GINGER

A PINCH OF GROUND CINNAMON

A PINCH OF GRATED NUTMEG

A PINCH OF FRESHLY GROUND BLACK PEPPER

2 TABLESPOONS CLEAR HONEY

Carefully wipe the duckling inside and out with a damp cloth and pat dry with kitchen paper.

Mix together the ingredients (except the honey) for the marinade. Spread the mixture over the inside and outside of the bird and wrap it completely in foil. Place the wrapped duckling in a refrigerator and leave for 24–36 hours. Remove it about two hours before cooking.

Preheat and prepare the barbecue for spit roasting, following the instructions on page 34.

Remove the duckling from the foil, reserving any remaining marinade. Run a spit through the exact centre of the bird, firmly set the spit forks in the thighs and breast and test for balance.

Position the spit on the barbecue and cook over medium heat if spit roasting with the barbecue lid down, or over medium to high heat if spit roasting with the lid open. Cook for about 1½ hours or until the thigh meat is soft when squeezed (protect the fingers with kitchen paper). Baste occasionally with the reserved marinade. Stir the honey into the marinade 15 minutes before the end of cooking and baste the duckling several times with the mixture so the skin is richly glazed. Carve and serve immediately.

Redskin wild duck

Although game butchers will supply the ducks well hung and ready to cook, they still need to be carefully wiped, inside and out, with a slightly damp cloth just before cooking. If the ducks are prepared at home, they will need to be plucked and singed, if necessary, and then the feet cut off at the first joint, the wings at the second and the neck fairly close to the body. Once drawn, their cavities should be washed with cold water and then wiped dry with kitchen paper.

SERVES 4–8

4 WILD DUCKS EACH WEIGHING 500 g–1.1 kg (1–2½ lb), WELL HUNG

125 g (4 oz) BUTTER, SOFTENED

WORCESTERSHIRE SAUCE FOR COATING

PAPRIKA FOR SPRINKLING

1½ TABLESPOONS CORNFLOUR

2–3 TABLESPOONS PORT

Preheat and prepare the barbecue for indirect heat cooking, following the instructions on page 33.

Rub the entire duck skins lightly with the butter. Place the ducks, head to tail, on a rack (if you have one) set in a roasting tin that will sit comfortably on just one half of the barbecue's grill area. Apply several shots of Worcestershire sauce over each duck and then sprinkle with sufficient paprika to completely coat the birds' breasts.

Cook, with medium to high heat, until the ducks are cooked to the desired degree. Depending on the weight of the individual ducks, and the way you like them cooked, this could take 25–75 minutes.

Remove the ducks and let them sit for a few minutes. If they are large, cut them in half with poultry shears to double up the servings. Take out the rack and carefully spoon off all the fat from the tin.

To make the gravy, blend the cornflour with the port and add to the tin juices. Place the tin over the lit side of the barbecue grill and, with high heat, bring the gravy to the boil, stirring constantly. Boil for a minute or so, still stirring.

Spoon some of the rich sauce over the ducks and serve the remainder separately.

Barbecued pheasant with wine sauce

Pheasant should be hung for at least three days for a decent flavour to develop and the meat to become tender. Hens (with the dull brown plumage) are plumper and more succulent than cock birds, and are generally considered to make better eating.

SERVES 2–4

1 PLUMP PHEASANT, WELL HUNG

3 TABLESPOONS SOFT BUTTER

3 SLICES OF STREAKY BACON

3 TABLESPOONS PORT OR RED WINE

1 GARLIC CLOVE, CHOPPED FINELY

SALT AND FRESHLY GROUND BLACK PEPPER

Preheat and prepare the barbecue for indirect heat cooking, following the instructions on page 33 (use a drip pan).

Carefully wipe the pheasant inside and out with a damp cloth. Spread the butter over the outside of the bird and wrap the slices of bacon around it. Cover the wing tips and the knuckle ends of the legs with foil. Season with salt and pepper.

Cook, with medium heat, for 1–1¼ hours, removing the bacon during the last 15 minutes of cooking to allow the breast to brown. To check that the pheasant is cooked, press the plumpest part of a thigh – it should feel soft.

Place the pheasant on a warm platter and leave it to rest for a few minutes before carving. Lift out the drip pan and stir the port or red wine and chopped garlic into it. Heat the port or wine mixture over the barbecue and serve as a sauce with the pheasant.

Grilled marinated quail

Unlike pheasant, quail should be eaten really fresh, preferably within twenty-four hours of being killed. This recipe calls for three quail per serving: two quail per head should still be adequate, but one quail per guest only stirs the appetite without satisfying it.

SERVES 4

12 QUAIL, DRAWN AND SPLIT LENGTHWAYS THROUGH THE BREAST-BONE

125 g (4 oz) BUTTER, MELTED

MARINADE

600 ml (1 PINT) DRY WHITE WINE

3 TABLESPOONS LEMON JUICE

1½ TABLESPOONS RED OR WHITE WINE VINEGAR

3 GARLIC CLOVES, CRUSHED

1 TEASPOON DRIED WHOLE TARRAGON OR ROSEMARY LEAVES

1 TEASPOON DRIED THYME

1 BAY LEAF

1 TEASPOON SALT

¼ TEASPOON FRESHLY GROUND BLACK PEPPER

To make the marinade, mix together the ingredients in a large saucepan and heat until simmering. Remove the pan from the heat, cover and allow to stand for 1–2 hours.

Pour the marinade into a dish and add the quail to the mixture, turning the birds over a few times before covering. Refrigerate for 6–8 hours or overnight.

Preheat and prepare the barbecue for grilling, following the instructions on page 30.

Remove the quail from the marinade, drain and then pat dry. (Either discard the marinade or freeze it for future use.)

Grill the quail, cut side down, over medium heat for about 15–20 minutes, turning them occasionally and basting them when you do so with the melted butter. Serve immediately.

Venison steaks with sauce

SERVES 4–6

750 g–1 kg (1½–2 lb) LOIN OF VENISON, BONED AND TIED

SALT PORK OR FAT BACON FOR LARDING (OPTIONAL)

SOFTENED BUTTER FOR BASTING

1 TABLESPOON JUNIPER BERRIES, CRUSHED

MARINADE

250 ml (8 fl oz) DRY RED WINE

1 MEDIUM-SIZE ONION, SLICED

1 MEDIUM-SIZE CARROT, SLICED

1 LARGE BOUQUET GARNI

2 TABLESPOONS OLIVE OIL

1 TABLESPOON RED OR WHITE WINE VINEGAR

6–8 BLACK PEPPERCORNS

SAUCE

2 TABLESPOONS OIL

2 SHALLOTS OR 1 SMALL ONION, CHOPPED FINELY

1 SMALL CARROT, CHOPPED FINELY

½ CELERY STICK, CHOPPED

1 TABLESPOON PLAIN FLOUR

450 ml (¾ PINT) BEEF BONE STOCK

1 TABLESPOON CRANBERRY JELLY

Cut the rolled loin into steaks (they look similar to tournedos) 2.5–4 cm (1–1½ inches) thick. Lard these steaks with salt pork or fat bacon, if desired.

To make the marinade, mix together the ingredients in a pan, bring to the boil and then leave until cold.

Place the steaks in a shallow dish and pour over the cold marinade. Cover the dish and leave for 6–8 hours or overnight in the refrigerator. If refrigerated, remove about 2 hours before cooking.

To prepare the sauce, heat the oil in a pan, add the shallots or onion, carrot and celery and cook until lightly coloured. Stir in the flour and cook slowly until the vegetables are nicely browned. Gradually stir in the stock and cook gently for about 30 minutes. Skim and strain the sauce. Then return it to the pan and continue simmering.

Preheat and prepare the barbecue for grilling, following the instructions on page 30.

Remove the steaks from the marinade, reserving the marinade, and dry them with kitchen paper. Strain the marinade into the sauce and let it continue to simmer, skimming any scum from the surface. Add the cranberry jelly and continue simmering until the sauce is syrupy.

Meanwhile, sear the steaks over high heat for about 10 seconds on each side. Move the steaks to the sides of the grill. Reduce the heat to low/medium and continue grilling the steaks, basting frequently with softened butter, for a further 3–4 minutes on each side, adding the juniper berries as you turn them, until cooked to the desired degree.

Spoon a little of the sauce over the venison steaks and serve immediately. Serve the remaining sauce separately.

*Spit-roasted
saddle or loin
of venison*
Page 93

Teriyaki
turkey drumsticks
Page 85

Streaky
drumsticks
Page 84

*Swordfish
steaks à la Niçoise*
Page 96

*Grilled
oysters with garlic
butter*
Page 100

Tandoori
fish
Page 94

Stir-fried
Szechuan prawns
Page 101

Spit-roasted saddle or loin of venison

Pictured on page 89
Gooseberry or redcurrant jelly make ideal accompaniments to this dish.

SERVES 6–8

1.75–2.25 kg (4–5 lb) SADDLE OR LOIN OF VENISON, TRIMMED OF FAT

125 g (4 oz) SALT PORK, CUT INTO THIN STRIPS

2 GARLIC CLOVES, EACH CUT INTO 4 SLIVERS

BASTING SAUCE

175 g (6 oz) CLEAR HONEY

150 ml (¼ PINT) SOY SAUCE

300 ml (½ PINT) ORANGE JUICE

JUICE OF 1 LEMON, STRAINED

150 ml (¼ PINT) TOMATO KETCHUP

300 ml (½ PINT) RED WINE VINEGAR

1 TEASPOON SALT

½ TEASPOON FRESHLY GROUND BLACK PEPPER

1 TEASPOON MUSTARD POWDER

½ TEASPOON PAPRIKA

Preheat and prepare the barbecue for spit roasting, following the instructions on page 34.

Wipe the venison with a damp cloth. Make slits in the meat and lard generously with the salt pork. Push the garlic slivers into the slits.

In a small pan mix together the honey, soy sauce, orange and lemon juice, tomato ketchup, wine vinegar, salt, pepper, mustard and paprika over low heat until blended.

Place the roast on the spit, balance it and secure firmly with the spit forks. Brush the venison generously with the basting sauce and cook over medium heat if spit roasting with the barbecue lid down, or over medium to high heat if the lid is open, until a meat thermometer inserted into the thickest part reads 60°C/140°F for rare meat or 85°C/185°F for well-done meat.

Fish & shellfish

Tickled trout

Tickling trout is no laughing matter for fish or fisherman. The trout I tickled and caught as a very young boy was all of 10 cm (4 inches) long.

SERVES 4

4 × 375 g (12 oz) TROUT, CLEANED AND BONED

OIL FOR BRUSHING

2 TABLESPOONS MELTED BUTTER

1 QUANTITY OF MAÎTRE D'HÔTEL BUTTER (PAGE 133), SOFTENED

MARINADE

3 TABLESPOONS OLIVE OIL

1 MEDIUM-SIZE ONION, CHOPPED FINELY

1 TEASPOON FRENCH MUSTARD

1 TABLESPOON VERY FINELY CHOPPED CHIVES

2 TABLESPOONS VERY FINELY CHOPPED DILL

1 TEASPOON SALT

1 TEASPOON LEMON JUICE

½ TEASPOON FRESHLY GROUND BLACK PEPPER

Remove the heads from the trout, if desired. Flatten the fish and place them flesh-side down in a shallow dish.

Combine the oil, onion, mustard, chives, dill, salt, lemon juice and pepper and mix thoroughly. Pour this marinade over the fish, cover and refrigerate for about an hour, turning the fish once.

Preheat and prepare the barbecue for grilling, following the instructions on page 30.

Brush oil over the inner surfaces of broilers. Alternatively, brush oil over the cooking grill.

Place the fish, flesh side down, into the broilers, or straight on to the grill, and cook over medium heat for about 4 minutes. Turn the fish over and brush the melted butter over the cooked side. Continue grilling for a further 5–6 minutes, or until the skin is crisp and the flesh white and easily flaked.

Spread the Maître d'Hôtel butter over the fish just before serving.

Tandoori fish

Pictured on page 92

SERVES 2–3

75 g (3 oz) BUTTER, MELTED

½ TEASPOON GROUND NUTMEG

1½ TEASPOONS GROUND CINNAMON

1½ TEASPOONS GROUND CORIANDER

JUICE OF 1½ LEMONS, STRAINED

1 WHOLE WHITE FISH WEIGHING 1 kg (2 lb), e.g. HADDOCK, COD OR OTHER WHITE, FIRM-FLESHED FISH

1 MEDIUM-SIZE ONION, CHOPPED FINELY

4 GARLIC CLOVES, CHOPPED VERY FINELY

2.5 cm (1-INCH) PIECE OF FRESH ROOT GINGER, PEELED AND CHOPPED FINELY

1 TEASPOON GROUND CUMIN

¼ TEASPOON CHILLI POWDER

1 TEASPOON GROUND FENNEL

½ TEASPOON PAPRIKA

1 TEASPOON SALT

¼ TEASPOON FRESHLY GROUND BLACK PEPPER

150 ml (¼ PINT) NATURAL YOGURT

First make the basting sauce. Combine the melted butter, nutmeg, ½ teaspoon of the cinnamon, ½ teaspoon of the coriander and the juice of half a lemon. Blend well and put aside.

Clean the fish; then make three diagonal incisions on each side.

Put the onion, garlic, ginger, cumin, remaining cinnamon and coriander, the chilli, fennel, paprika, salt, pepper and the remaining lemon juice in a food processor (or, preferably, use a pestle and mortar) and blend to make a paste. Stir in the yogurt.

Rub the mixture on the inside and outside of the fish and leave in a cool place for 3–4 hours.

Preheat and prepare the barbecue for spit roasting or grilling, following the instructions on page 34 or 30.

Mount the fish securely on a spit, preferably within a spit-mounted, double-hinged fish broiler, or grill using a large, hinged fish broiler (grilling basket). Cook the fish over medium heat, basting frequently with the basting sauce, for 15 minutes if spit roasting or 7–8 minutes per side if grilling.

Baked whole fish

This recipe can be used for sea bass, salmon or red mullet.

SERVES 6–12

1 WHOLE FISH WEIGHING 1.75–3 kg (4–7 lb), CLEANED AND SCALED IF NECESSARY

4 SPRING ONIONS, CHOPPED VERY FINELY

1 TEASPOON SALT

1 TEASPOON SUGAR

1 TEASPOON FRESHLY GRATED ROOT GINGER

1 TABLESPOON SOY SAUCE

1 TABLESPOON SAKE, DRY SHERRY OR DRY WINE

1 TABLESPOON GROUNDNUT OR 2 TEASPOONS SESAME OIL, PLUS EXTRA FOR BRUSHING

Wipe the fish inside and out with a damp cloth and pat dry with kitchen paper. Remove the fins but leave the head and tail intact unless you object strongly to leaving the head on. Score the fish, almost to the bone, with 3 parallel diagonal slashes, on each side.

Combine the spring onions, salt, sugar, ginger, soy sauce, sake, sherry or wine and chosen oil. Rub the fish inside and out with this mixture. Allow the fish to stand, in a cool place, for 30 minutes.

Preheat and prepare the barbecue for indirect heat cooking, following the instructions on page 33.

If you have a fish broiler large enough

to accommodate the fish, brush the inside of the cage with oil before enclosing the fish. Alternatively, make an aluminium pan (see Tools and Accessories) large enough for the fish. Brush the inside surface of the pan with oil before adding the fish.

Cook the fish with high heat. If using a fish broiler, allow 10 minutes total cooking time for every 2.5 cm (1 inch) of the fish's thickness (at its thickest point). Allow 2–3 minutes extra per 2.5 cm (1 inch) if cooking the fish in a foil pan. Brush frequently with groundnut oil during cooking and carefully turn the fish halfway through cooking. When the fish is done the skin will be nicely browned and the flesh easily flaked with a fork. Do not overcook!

Fish steaks with sweet and sour sauce

SERVES 6

6 FRESH OR FROZEN HALIBUT, HADDOCK, COD OR SWORDFISH STEAKS, 2.5 cm (1 INCH) THICK

OIL FOR GREASING

SWEET AND SOUR SAUCE

150 ml (¼ PINT) DRY WHITE WINE

2 TABLESPOONS WHITE WINE VINEGAR

2 TABLESPOONS OIL

300 ml (½ PINT) CRUSHED PINEAPPLE WITH JUICE

1 TABLESPOON SOY SAUCE

2 TEASPOONS LEMON JUICE

½ TEASPOON MUSTARD POWDER

½ TEASPOON GARLIC SALT

1½ TABLESPOONS BROWN SUGAR

1 TABLESPOON CHOPPED ONION (OPTIONAL)

Thaw the steaks if frozen. Arrange the fish steaks in a shallow dish.

Mix together the ingredients for the sauce. Pour the sauce over the steaks, cover and leave in the refrigerator for 30 minutes, turning once.

Preheat and prepare the barbecue for grilling or indirect heat cooking, following the instructions on page 30 or 33.

Briefly drain the fish and reserve the sauce. Place the fish steaks in an oiled wire broiler or on an oiled grill and cook, over medium heat, for 5 minutes each side or until the fish flakes easily with a fork, basting with the sauce several times during cooking.

Alternatively, arrange the steaks in a shallow baking tin, baste with the sauce and cook by the indirect heat method, allowing an extra 8–10 minutes total cooking time. Turn over the steaks carefully about half-way through cooking and baste them with the sauce.

Grilled salmon steaks

SERVES 4

4 SALMON STEAKS ABOUT 2.5 cm (1 INCH) THICK

1 TEASPOON VERY FINELY CHOPPED ONION

½ TEASPOON PAPRIKA

A GENEROUS PINCH OF GARLIC SALT

2 TEASPOONS LEMON JUICE

OIL OR MELTED BUTTER FOR BRUSHING

SALT AND FRESHLY GROUND WHITE PEPPER

Wipe the fish with a damp cloth. Season both sides of the salmon steaks with salt and pepper.

Stir the onion, paprika, garlic salt and a little more pepper to taste, into the lemon juice. Brush both sides of the salmon steaks with the marinade and leave in a cool place for about 30 minutes. Drain briefly, reserving any liquid.

Preheat and prepare the barbecue for grilling, following the instructions on page 30.

If using a hinged broiler, brush oil over the inside. Place the steaks inside and cook over medium to high heat for 6–7 minutes each side, basting frequently with any leftover marinade.

Alternatively, tear off four pieces of 46 cm (18-inch) heavy-duty foil each large enough to make a generous parcel round each steak. Brush melted butter on the shiny side of each piece. Place a prepared steak in the centre of one of the buttered surfaces, add a little leftover marinade if wished and bring the two long sides together above the steak. Fold over twice (leaving space for heat circulation and expansion); then fold the short ends in the same way to make a fairly leak-proof package. Do this with the other steaks and pieces of foil. Place the packages on the grill and cook, over medium to high heat, for about 10 minutes each side or until the fish flakes easily.

Swordfish steaks à la Niçoise

Pictured on page 91

If swordfish is not available, substitute another firm-fleshed fish such as shark, halibut, turbot or cod.

SERVES 4

4 × 250 g (8 oz) SWORDFISH STEAKS

OIL FOR BRUSHING

SAUCE

4 TABLESPOONS SOFT BUTTER

2 TABLESPOONS OLIVE OIL

2 GARLIC CLOVES, CHOPPED VERY FINELY

2 ANCHOVY FILLETS, SOAKED, DRAINED AND MASHED

1 TABLESPOON FINELY CHOPPED FRESH PARSLEY

3 BLACK OLIVES, STONED AND CHOPPED FINELY (OPTIONAL)

JUICE OF 1 LEMON, STRAINED

FRESHLY GROUND BLACK PEPPER

GARNISH

LEMON WEDGES

COARSELY CHOPPED FRESH PARSLEY

Preheat and prepare the barbecue for grilling, following the instructions on page 30.

To make the sauce, melt the butter in a small saucepan. Add the oil, garlic, anchovy fillets, parsley, olives, if using, and lemon juice. Add pepper to taste. Cook over low to medium heat for 10 minutes, stirring occasionally. Keep the pan over very low heat until ready to use.

Brush the swordfish steaks with oil and grill over high heat for 6–10 minutes per side, depending on the thickness of the steaks. Take care not to overcook.

Pour the sauce evenly over the 4 steaks and garnish with lemon wedges and chopped parsley.

Grilled red mullet with fennel

Pictured on the front cover

The marvellous flavour of the fish will be enhanced during cooking if you leave the liver inside the fish. Once the fish is cooked the liver can be extracted carefully and then pounded with a tablespoon of chopped capers, a tablespoon of chopped oregano, and 3 to 4 tablespoons of olive oil. This makes a very tasty salad dressing.

To further increase the aromatic flavour of the fish, place a handful of dried fennel stalks on the hot rocks just before grilling it. The resulting scented smoke will also stimulate appetites!

SERVES 4

4 LARGE OR 8 SMALL RED MULLET

MARINADE

1 TABLESPOON MELTED BUTTER

2 TABLESPOONS OIL

½ TEASPOON BLACK PEPPERCORNS, CRACKED

2 TABLESPOONS DRY WHITE OR RED WINE

2 GARLIC CLOVES, CHOPPED FINELY

3 LARGE BAY LEAVES, EACH BROKEN INTO 4 PIECES

1½ TABLESPOONS CHOPPED FRESH FENNEL LEAVES

Clean the fish, but leave the liver (a delicacy of excellent flavour) intact. Make two deep cuts on each side of each fish. Mix together the ingredients for the marinade and pour over the fish. Marinate for about 1 hour.

Preheat and prepare the barbecue for grilling, following the instructions on page 30.

Drain the fish, reserving the marinade, and grill over medium to high heat for 5–8 minutes on each side, depending on the size and thickness of the fish. Baste each side of the fish twice during cooking with the reserved marinade.

Mackerel parmesan

SERVES 4

4 FRESH MACKEREL EACH WEIGHING ABOUT 300 g (10 oz)

OIL FOR GREASING

MARINADE

125 ml (4 fl oz) OIL

4 TABLESPOONS LEMON JUICE

2 TABLESPOONS CHOPPED FRESH PARSLEY

½ TEASPOON DRIED BASIL

½ TEASPOON SALT

¼ TEASPOON FRESHLY GROUND WHITE PEPPER

COATING

75 g (3 oz) PARMESAN CHEESE, GRATED

25 g (1 oz) DRY WHITE BREADCRUMBS

½ TEASPOON GARLIC SALT

Clean and rinse the mackerel thoroughly inside and out under cold running water and wipe dry with kitchen paper. Place the fish side by side in a shallow dish.

Mix together the oil, lemon juice, parsley, basil, salt and pepper for the marinade. Pour the marinade over the fish, cover and keep in the refrigerator for 1 hour, turning the fish once or twice.

Preheat and prepare the barbecue for grilling, following the instructions on page 30.

Lift the fish from the marinade, drain briefly and reserve the marinade.

In a shallow dish combine the cheese, breadcrumbs and garlic salt. Thickly cover the fish with the cheese mixture, pressing it on to the skin. Drizzle the fish with some of the reserved marinade. Place in oiled fish broilers on a well-oiled grill and cook, over medium heat, for about 5 minutes. Turn the fish and cook for a further 5–6 minutes or until the flesh flakes easily when prodded with a fork in the thickest part. Baste the fish frequently with the reserved marinade during cooking.

Note: the given timings are based on a fish

measuring 2.5 cm (1 inch) at the thickest part. Use the same ratio: 10 minutes total cooking time per 2.5 cm (1 inch) of thickness for fish of varying thickness; therefore a fish 5 cm (2 inches) thick should be cooked for 20 minutes (10 minutes each side).

Herring grilled with fresh herbs

A fish that is at its best in the summer. The dish is delicately flavoured, but beware of the bones.

SERVES 4

4 MEDIUM-SIZE FRESH HERRING, CLEANED

125 g (4 oz) BUTTER

¼ TEASPOON GROUND CARDAMOM

½ TEASPOON GROUND CORIANDER

½ TEASPOON SALT

A GOOD PINCH OF FRESHLY GROUND BLACK PEPPER

300 ml (½ PINT) NATURAL YOGURT

OIL FOR BRUSHING

SPRIGS OF FRESH FENNEL, DILL OR THYME

Scrape the fish to remove all the scales, discard the heads and trim the tails. Make three diagonal cuts across each side of the body. Pat the fish dry with kitchen paper.

Preheat and prepare the barbecue for grilling, following the instructions on page 30.

Melt the butter in a small saucepan and stir in the cardamom, coriander, salt, pepper and yogurt. Brush the fish generously, inside and out, with the seasoned butter.

Place the fish in oiled individual or multiple fish broilers – hinged grilling baskets. (An oiled rectangular steak or hamburger broiler will suffice, providing it is large enough to accommodate the fish.) Otherwise, place the fish directly on to a well oiled grill.

Cook the fish, over high heat, for 5–7 minutes each side until the skin is crisp and the flesh flakes easily with a fork, basting the fish frequently with the seasoned butter and placing sprigs of the chosen fresh herb on the hot rocks throughout.

Heat any remaining seasoned butter and serve with the fish.

Sardines asadas with herb and garlic butter

To impart that little bit of extra oceanic flavour to the cleaned sardines, bury them in coarse salt and leave to cure for 1–2 hours. Brush off most of the salt before proceeding to oil, season and grill the fish. Frozen sardines may be used, but thaw them thoroughly beforehand.

SERVES 4

20 SMALL FRESH SARDINES, CLEANED

4 TABLESPOONS OLIVE OIL, PLUS EXTRA FOR GREASING

SALT AND FRESHLY GROUND BLACK PEPPER

1 QUANTITY OF HERB AND GARLIC BUTTER (PAGE 133), TO SERVE

Preheat and prepare the barbecue for grilling, following the instructions on page 30.

Pat the fish dry. Brush lightly with the oil and season to taste with salt and pepper. Place the fish on a well-oiled grill and cook, over high heat, for about 5 minutes each side.

Serve the sardines with pats of the Herb and Garlic Butter.

Smoky grilled mussels

Do not let the fact that mussels are only generally available between September and March put you off trying this simple, inexpensive and delicious recipe. Mussels are best eaten on the day of purchase, but if you have to keep them overnight, do so (having washed and scrubbed them) in a bucket full of salted water. Sprinkle some fine oatmeal over the water and leave the bucket in a cool place covered with a damp tea towel.

Mussels are just about my favourite shellfish – in fact it would be true to say that I'm a fool over the *moule*!

SERVES 4

40–50 MUSSELS

A LARGE BUNCH OF DRIED HERBS, e.g. ROSEMARY, THYME, etc.

1 QUANTITY OF HERB AND GARLIC BUTTER OR GARLIC BUTTER (PAGE 133), MELTED

Place the mussels under running cold water for at least 30 minutes.

Preheat and prepare the barbecue for grilling, following the instructions on page 30.

Scrape away any weed and clean the mussels by scrubbing with a small stiff brush.

Place the mussels in a single layer on the grill and cook over medium to medium/high heat. Scatter the dried herbs on to the hot rocks throughout the short cooking period (keeping the lid closed will enhance the effect of the scented smoke). When the mussels have opened fully, leave them on the grill for another minute. Discard any shells that have failed to open.

Serve immediately, with the melted Herb and Garlic or Garlic Butter.

Mussels with herb and garlic stuffing

SERVES 4

2.25 LITRES (4 PINTS) MUSSELS

125 g (4 oz) BUTTER, AT ROOM TEMPERATURE

1 HEAPED TABLESPOON CHOPPED FRESH PARSLEY

2 GARLIC CLOVES, CRUSHED

1 TABLESPOON LEMON JUICE

SALT AND FRESHLY GROUND BLACK PEPPER

Place the mussels under running cold water for at least 30 minutes. Scrape away any weed and then clean by scrubbing with a small stiff brush.

Preheat and prepare the barbecue for grilling, following the instructions on page 30.

Put the prepared mussels into a large pan, cover with a lid and cook on the grill over medium heat until they open (it is unnecessary to add liquid at this stage). Remove and discard the empty half shells and any shells that have failed to open.

While the mussels are cooking, combine the butter, parsley, garlic, lemon juice and salt and pepper in a basin and mix well.

Prepare the barbecue for indirect heat cooking, following the instructions on page 33. Arrange the mussels in their half shells on a baking tray. Spoon a small amount of the butter mixture on to each mussel and cook, with medium to medium/high heat, for 5–10 minutes.

Serve immediately, with chunks of fresh bread to mop up the juices.

Angels on horseback

SERVES 4

8 CANNED OR RAW OYSTERS, SHELLED

1 TABLESPOON LEMON JUICE

8 THIN RASHERS OF BACON

MELTED BUTTER FOR BRUSHING

SALT AND FRESHLY GROUND BLACK PEPPER

4 SLICES OF HOT, BUTTERED TOAST, TO SERVE

Soak 8 wooden cocktail sticks in water, if using. Preheat and prepare the barbecue for grilling, following the instructions on page 30.

Sprinkle the oysters with the lemon juice and salt and pepper. Wrap each oyster in a bacon rasher and fasten with a soaked wooden cocktail stick or fine metal skewer.

Brush the skewered oysters with melted butter and grill, over medium to medium/high heat, for about 4 minutes, turning them several times. Serve immediately, with the prepared toast.

Grilled oysters with garlic butter

Pictured on page 91

Before buying your oysters, I strongly recommend that you are in possession of an oyster knife!

SERVES 4

24 OYSTERS

250 g (8 oz) BUTTER

2 TEASPOONS VERY FINELY CHOPPED GARLIC

3 TABLESPOONS VERY FINELY CHOPPED FRESH PARSLEY

JUICE OF 1 LEMON

Scrub the oysters well and keep them, flat shell uppermost, covered with a damp cloth in a bucket until ready to cook. Do not store in water.

Preheat and prepare the barbecue for grilling, following the instructions on page 30.

Mix together the butter, garlic, parsley and lemon juice in a saucepan and place so it simmers gently on the grill just before cooking the oysters.

Open the oysters, preferably using an oyster knife, and remove the flat shell. Cut the oysters loose from their bottom shells. Add a teaspoonful or so of the garlic butter to each oyster.

Place the shells in a single layer on the grill and cook over high heat until the juices in the shells are bubbling and the oysters beginning to shrink. (The exact cooking time will depend on personal preference, but overcooking will make the oysters chewy!)

Serve immediately.

Special baked scallops

SERVES 4

25 g (1 oz) BUTTER, MELTED

6 LARGE SCALLOPS, SHELLS REMOVED, WASHED AND DRIED

1 LEMON, HALVED

5 TABLESPOONS DOUBLE CREAM

3 TABLESPOONS FRESH BREADCRUMBS

SALT AND FRESHLY GROUND BLACK PEPPER

Preheat and prepare the barbecue for indirect heat cooking, following the instructions on page 33.

Put 1 teaspoon of the melted butter in the bottom of 4 of the shells. Quarter the scallops and place 6 pieces in each shell. Season with salt and pepper and add a good squeeze of lemon juice. Spoon over the cream and sprinkle with the breadcrumbs. Dribble the rest of the melted butter over the breadcrumbs.

Bake, with medium to medium/high heat, for 8–10 minutes or until the tops are golden brown.

Stir-fried Szechuan prawns

Pictured on page 92

SERVES 2

500 g (1 lb) MEDIUM-SIZE RAW PRAWNS

2 SPRING ONIONS, CHOPPED COARSELY

2 × 2.5 cm (1-INCH) PIECE OF FRESH ROOT GINGER,
PEELED AND CRUSHED

50 g (2 oz) MANGETOUT OR FRENCH BEANS, CUT INTO
5 cm (2-INCH) LENGTHS

½ TEASPOON SESAME OIL

3 TABLESPOONS RICE WINE OR DRY SHERRY

1 TEASPOON SUGAR

6 TABLESPOONS SOY SAUCE

1 DRIED HOT RED PEPPER, DE-SEEDED AND
CRUSHED

2 TABLESPOONS VEGETABLE OIL

Pull away the legs from the prawns. Carefully de-vein the prawns by slitting the shell down the back (try not to dislodge the shell whilst removing the black threadlike vein). Rinse the prawns quickly in cold water.

Combine all the remaining ingredients, except the vegetable oil, in a dish. Add the prawns to the marinade, cover the dish, and leave in the refrigerator for 2–3 hours, stirring occasionally.

Preheat and prepare the barbecue for wok-cooking, following the instructions on page 38.

Remove the prawns from the marinade, drain them, pat dry with kitchen paper, and reserve the marinade.

Place the wok on the barbecue and heat the vegetable oil. When hot, add the prawns and stir-fry, over high heat, for 3–4 minutes. Do not overcook, the prawns are done when they turn a pink colour.

Pour in the reserved marinade, bring rapidly to the boil and serve the prawns immediately.

Grilled lobster

Fresh lobster is available during the spring/summer months. Females not only make better eating but also provide the coral for making delicious coral butter.

SERVES 2

2 LIVE FEMALE LOBSTERS EACH WEIGHING ABOUT
500 g (1 lb)

175 g (6 oz) BUTTER

1 TEASPOON PAPRIKA

SALT AND FRESHLY GROUND BLACK PEPPER

1 LEMON, CUT INTO WEDGES, TO SERVE

Kill the lobsters by laying them on their backs and inserting the tip of a sharp knife between the body shell and tail segment – thus severing the spinal cord. Otherwise, plunge each lobster head first into vigorously boiling water, using tongs to hold it under the surface for 2–3 minutes (the lobster will begin to turn red).

Preheat and prepare the barbecue for grilling, following the instructions on page 30.

Place the lobsters on a cutting board and split lengthways by drawing a sharp knife down the centre of the back. Discard the black intestine running down the middle of the tail and the white gills from the top of the head. Remove the bright red coral or roe and keep to one side.

Mix together 50 g (2 oz) of the butter, the paprika, and a pinch each of salt and pepper. Spread over the lobster flesh.

Grill the lobsters, cut side down, over medium to medium/high heat, for 5–7 minutes. Turn the lobster halves and cook for 10 minutes or so. (By doing this the lobster's shell will retain most of the meat juices.) The lobster is ready to eat when the tail meat becomes opaque.

Blend the remaining butter with the reserved coral or roe. Serve the lobsters with the coral butter and the lemon wedges.

Vegetables

Gem squash à Nolan

Pictured on page 109

Judy Nolan, an old family friend, fell in love with this exotic vegetable during her photographic safari to Africa. A first-class cook and practising barbecuer, this is Judy's recipe for a vegetable which is now a regular feature in supermarkets and greengrocers.

SERVES 1–2

1 GEM SQUASH

50 g (2 oz) BUTTER

SALT AND FRESHLY GROUND BLACK PEPPER

Preheat and prepare the barbecue for grilling or indirect heat cooking, following the instructions on page 30 or 33.

Remove the stem, and then cut the squash in half crossways and scoop out the seeds. Place half the butter in each half. Season lightly with salt and a generous amount of pepper.

Place each half in the centre of a square of heavy-duty foil roughly three times the diameter of the vegetable. Bring the four corners of the foil together into a pyramid shape. Loosely fold over the foil edges where they meet to seal. Keep the package upright and grill, over high heat, for about 15 minutes; or roast – using the indirect heat method – for 25–30 minutes.

Orange and ginger glazed carrots

The orange juice and ginger, combined with the butter or honey, makes an attractive and tasty glaze which combines well with the flavour of carrot. For a more tangy taste, replace the ginger with Worcestershire sauce.

SERVES 4–6

1 kg (2 lb) NEW CARROTS

2 ORANGES

2 TEASPOONS FRESHLY GRATED ROOT GINGER OR ½ TEASPOON GROUND GINGER

75 g (3 oz) BUTTER OR 2 TABLESPOONS CLEAR HONEY

SALT

Parboil the carrots in boiling, lightly salted water until just tender but still crisp. Drain well. Grate the zest from the oranges and squeeze out the juice.

Preheat and prepare the barbecue for grilling, following the instructions on page 30.

Combine the orange zest, orange juice, ginger, butter or honey in a saucepan and, stirring constantly, bring the mixture to the boil. Simmer gently for about 5 minutes. Dip the carrots in the mixture, coating them completely.

Grill over medium heat for about 5 minutes, turning and basting the carrots occasionally with the remaining sauce. If using the honey glaze, turn the carrots more frequently to avoid excessive caramelisation.

Sweetcorn with dill

SERVES 6

6 YOUNG SWEETCORN COBS

125 g (4 oz) BUTTER, SOFTENED

1 TEASPOON DILL WEED

6 CORIANDER SEEDS, CRUSHED

1 TEASPOON SALT

A PINCH OF GRATED NUTMEG

Loosen the husks sufficiently to strip away the silk (see opposite). Soak the cobs in cold water for at least 30 minutes. When ready to cook, drain well.

Preheat and prepare the barbecue for grilling, following the instructions on page 30.

Blend together all the remaining ingredients and spread generously over the sweetcorn. Re-position the husks, place each cob on a sheet of aluminium foil and wrap securely. Cook by direct heat, over medium heat, for 15–20 minutes, turning several times.

Bacon-wrapped corn

SERVES 6

6 YOUNG SWEETCORN COBS

1 QUANTITY OF GARLIC BUTTER (PAGE 133), SOFTENED

6 RASHERS OF STREAKY BACON, RINDS REMOVED

SOFTENED BUTTER FOR BASTING

SALT

Remove the corn husks and silk (see above) and soak the corn for 30 minutes in salted, iced water. Soak 6 wooden cocktail sticks in water. When ready to cook, drain well.

Preheat and prepare the barbecue for grilling, following the instructions on page 30.

Spread the cobs generously with the Garlic Butter. Wrap a rasher of bacon around the length of each corn and secure with the soaked wooden cocktail sticks. Grill over medium heat for about 25 minutes, turning frequently and basting any large uncovered areas with softened butter, until the bacon is crisp and the uncovered corn is golden brown.

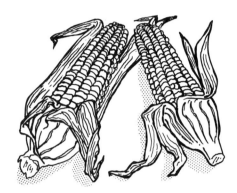

Sweetcorn with the husks pulled back

Pilau rice

This highly spiced rice dish, of Eastern origin, goes well with most meats – particularly kebabs.

SERVES 4

40 g (1½ oz) BUTTER

1 MEDIUM-SIZE ONION, CHOPPED FINELY

175 g (6 oz) LONG-GRAIN RICE, WASHED AND DRAINED

450 ml (¾ PINT) CHICKEN STOCK OR WATER

A PINCH OF SAFFRON POWDER OR TURMERIC

½ TEASPOON DRIED OREGANO

SALT AND FRESHLY GROUND BLACK PEPPER

Preheat and prepare the barbecue for indirect heat cooking, following the instructions on page 33.

Melt the butter in an ovenproof baking dish. Add the onion and cook until soft and slightly brown. Add the rice and cook, over moderate heat, for 2–3 minutes.

Stir in the chicken stock or water,

saffron powder or turmeric, oregano and salt and pepper to taste.

Cook, with low to medium heat, for 20–25 minutes or until all the liquid has been absorbed and the rice is fluffy and tender.

Barbecued baked beans

SERVES 4–6

125 g (4 oz) STREAKY BACON RASHERS, RINDS REMOVED

25 g (1 oz) BUTTER

1 TABLESPOON OIL

1 LARGE ONION, CHOPPED FINELY

1 CELERY STICK, CHOPPED FINELY

475 g (15 oz) CAN OF BAKED BEANS IN TOMATO SAUCE

4 SMALL FRANKFURTER SAUSAGES

1 TABLESPOON HORSERADISH SAUCE

2 TABLESPOONS WORCESTERSHIRE SAUCE

1 TEASPOON FRENCH MUSTARD

3 TABLESPOONS TOMATO KETCHUP

50 g (2 oz) SOFT DARK BROWN SUGAR

Preheat and prepare the barbecue for grilling, following the instructions on page 30.

Cut the rashers of bacon into pieces about 2.5 cm (1 inch) long. Put the bacon into a heavy-based saucepan and heat gently on the barbecue until the fat starts to run. Add the butter, oil, onion and celery and continue to cook gently until the onion is translucent and golden brown.

Put the remaining ingredients into the pan and heat through, stirring frequently. If you wish to give the beans a nice smoky flavour, drop a handful of soaked wood chips, such as hickory, or perhaps some fresh herbs, on to the hot rock early on during heating. With the lid down (in between stirring), the aromatic smoke will help to give a smoky flavour. Don't worry if the surface becomes a little dry – this will give a little extra tang to the beans and help evoke images of chuck-wagons of old trundling along the Chisholm Trail.

Cheese and herb stuffed tomatoes

The indirect heat method of cooking (page 33) gives the surface of the tomatoes a more appetising appearance, but the cooking time will need to be extended by several minutes.

SERVES 4

2 LARGE FIRM TOMATOES

3 TABLESPOONS FRESH WHITE BREADCRUMBS

2 TABLESPOONS FINELY CHOPPED FRESH PARSLEY

1 SMALL GARLIC CLOVE, CRUSHED

25 g (1 oz) GRATED CHEESE, e.g. CHEDDAR, MOZZARELLA, etc.

2 TABLESPOONS SOFT BUTTER

A PINCH OF DRIED BASIL

Preheat and prepare the barbecue for grilling, following the instructions on page 30.

Cut the tomatoes in half lengthways and scrape out the seeds using a teaspoon. Combine the remaining ingredients and lightly pack the mixture into the tomato cavities.

Place the tomato halves, cut side up, on the grill and cook, over medium heat, for about 10 minutes or until the tomatoes are heated through and the cheese has melted.

Tomatoes Provençale

SERVES 4–6

4 TABLESPOONS SOFT BUTTER

2 TABLESPOONS FINELY CHOPPED SHALLOTS

2 TABLESPOONS CHOPPED FRESH PARSLEY

½ TEASPOON DRIED TARRAGON

A PINCH OF DRIED BASIL

½ TEASPOON SUGAR

3 TABLESPOONS DRY WHITE WINE

4 MEDIUM-SIZE TOMATOES, PEELED AND QUARTERED

2 GARLIC CLOVES, CHOPPED VERY FINELY

SALT AND FRESHLY GROUND BLACK PEPPER

Preheat and prepare the barbecue for grilling, following the instructions on page 30.

Melt 2 tablespoons of the butter in a large skillet or heavy frying pan over high heat. Add the shallots, parsley, tarragon, basil, sugar and wine. Bring the mixture to the boil, stirring occasionally.

Add the tomatoes and stir gently until they are heated through. Add the remaining butter and the garlic and stir gently until the butter has melted. Remove immediately from the heat, season with salt and pepper and serve.

Ratatouille

I am still not sure if I prefer Ratatouille hot or cold, but it certainly goes well at any temperature with chicken, lamb, beef or fish.

SERVES 4–6

1 MEDIUM-SIZE AUBERGINE

2 MEDIUM–LARGE ONIONS

4 SMALL COURGETTES

1 MEDIUM-SIZE RED PEPPER, DE-SEEDED

1 MEDIUM-SIZE GREEN PEPPER, DE-SEEDED

2 TOMATOES

6 TABLESPOONS OIL

3 GARLIC CLOVES, CRUSHED

1 TABLESPOON CHOPPED FRESH BASIL OR 1 TEASPOON DRIED BASIL

1 TEASPOON DRIED ROSEMARY

1 BAY LEAF

1 TEASPOON SALT

½ TEASPOON FRESHLY GROUND BLACK PEPPER

2 TABLESPOONS CHOPPED FRESH PARSLEY

Preheat and prepare the barbecue for grilling, following the instructions on page 30.

Thinly slice the aubergine, onions and courgettes. Chop the red and green peppers. Remove the skins and seeds from the tomatoes and cut the flesh into wedges.

Place a large skillet on the grill and heat the oil over high heat. Add the onions and garlic and cook for about 5 minutes or until the onion is soft and translucent. Next add the aubergine, peppers and courgettes. Cook for another 5 minutes, shaking the skillet frequently.

Add the tomatoes, basil, rosemary, bay leaf, salt and pepper. Sprinkle over the parsley. Bring the lid of the barbecue down, reduce the heat to medium and continue cooking for a further 50–60 minutes. Serve the ratatouille hot or cold as a main dish or with chicken, lamb, fish or beef.

Note: if you do not have a large, cast-iron skillet, a large frying pan or wok could be substituted (use one with a heatproof handle and protect the pan end with 2 or 3 layers of foil). To help stabilise the wok, and also make it easier to bring the lid of the barbecue down, remove the food grill and nestle the wok in the unit's bottom casting.

Mixed vegetable kebabs

Pictured on the front cover
You may prefer to concentrate on one vegetable per skewer, although in doing so the small interchange of flavours created by different vegetables nestling together will be lost.

SERVES 6

6 VERY SMALL POTATOES, PREFERABLY NEW

6 SMALL ONIONS

12 SMALL CLOSED-CUP MUSHROOMS

1 LARGE GREEN PEPPER, DE-SEEDED

2 SMALL COURGETTES

OIL FOR GREASING

50 g (2 oz) BUTTER, MELTED

½ TEASPOON GARLIC SALT

¼ TEASPOON FRESHLY GROUND BLACK PEPPER

6 VERY SMALL, FIRM TOMATOES

SALT

Preheat and prepare the barbecue for grilling, following the instructions on page 30.

Cook the potatoes and onions separately in lightly salted, boiling water until they are barely tender.

Discard the stems from the mushrooms and wipe the caps. Cut the pepper into 6 pieces. Cut the courgettes into 6 pieces 2.5–4 cm (1–1½ inches) long. Drain the onions and potatoes, and thread all but the tomatoes alternately on to oiled (preferably flat-bladed) skewers.

Blend together the melted butter, garlic salt and pepper and brush the kebabs

generously with the mixture.

Cook, turning frequently and basting with the butter, over medium to high heat, for about 5 minutes. Add a tomato to each skewer and continue cooking, turning and basting, for a further 5 minutes.

Potato kebabs Madras

SERVES 4

750 g (1½ lb) POTATOES, CUT INTO 2.5–4 cm (1–1½-INCH) CUBES

OIL FOR GREASING

6 TABLESPOONS BOTTLED CURRY PASTE OR CURRY POWDER BLENDED WITH WATER

SALT

Cook the potato cubes in boiling, salted water until they are barely tender – a fine skewer should push into the potato without undue pressure. Drain thoroughly and, when cool enough to handle, thread the cubes on to oiled (preferably flat-bladed) skewers, leaving a small gap between each cube. Generously brush the cubes with the curry paste or blended curry powder and allow to stand for up to an hour.

Preheat and prepare the barbecue for grilling, following the instructions on page 30.

Grill over high heat for about 10 minutes or until the potato cubes are uniformly cooked on all sides. For those who prefer extra tangy kebabs, baste the potatoes once or twice during cooking with any leftover paste. Serve immediately.

Herb and sesame new potatoes

Pictured on page 109

SERVES 4–6

1 kg (2 lb) NEW POTATOES

50 g (2 oz) BUTTER

1 TABLESPOON CHOPPED FRESH PARSLEY

1 TABLESPOON CHOPPED FRESH MINT

1 TABLESPOON SEASAME SEEDS, TOASTED

SALT AND FRESHLY GROUND BLACK PEPPER

Peel a 2.5 cm (1-inch) strip from the circumference of each potato.

Preheat and prepare the barbecue for grilling or indirect heat cooking, following the instructions on page 30 or 33.

Grease a large piece of heavy-duty aluminium foil (or two layers of ordinary foil) with about half the butter. Place the potatoes together in the centre of the foil and season with salt and pepper. Sprinkle over some of the herbs. Wrap the foil securely around the potatoes, following one of the methods outlined on page 40.

Cook for 40–55 minutes, depending on the size of the potatoes and the cooking technique employed. Check that they are cooked by piercing the top of the foil pack and into the potatoes with a fine metal skewer. Open the foil, sprinkle the potatoes with the remaining herbs and sesame seeds and dot with the remaining butter before serving.

Baked potatoes with toppings

Select nicely shaped, even-size potatoes. Potatoes that are particularly good for baking include King Edward, Golden Wonder, Maris Piper and Pentland Ivory. The ingredients for the toppings need to be well mixed before they are added to the potatoes.

SERVES 4

4 MEDIUM/LARGE POTATOES

GROUNDNUT OR SESAME OIL

SALT AND FRESHLY GROUND BLACK PEPPER OR
BARBECUE SPICE

Preheat and prepare the barbecue for grilling or indirect heat cooking, following the instructions on page 30 or 33.

Scrub the potatoes well, pat dry and prick deeply all over with a skewer or fork. Brush with oil. (I find it easier, when tackling several potatoes, to use my hands.) Season with salt and pepper or sprinkle generously with barbecue spice. Wrap the potatoes in foil or, if you like a crispy skin, leave the potatoes unwrapped.

Cook by direct heat, over medium to high heat, and turn the potatoes several times during cooking (a medium-size potato will take 45–60 minutes and a large one 60–70 minutes). Alternatively, bake the potatoes by the indirect heat method, perhaps alongside a joint of meat. (This takes longer and it is a good idea to turn the potatoes over roughly half-way through cooking.)

Cut a cross in the top of each potato and pinch to open out the centre. Top with any of the following toppings.

CREAM CHEESE AND CRISPY BACON

125 g (4 oz) CREAM CHEESE OR GRATED CHEDDAR
CHEESE

175 g (6 oz) CRISPLY GRILLED BACK BACON,
CRUMBLED

50 g (2 oz) BUTTER

2 TABLESPOONS FINELY CHOPPED FRESH CHIVES

2 TEASPOONS FINELY CHOPPED RED PEPPER, TO
GARNISH

CHEESE, PICKLE AND SAUSAGE

75 g (3 oz) GRATED CHEDDAR CHEESE

3 TABLESPOONS SWEET PICKLE, CHOPPED IF
NECESSARY

4 COOKED PORK CHIPOLATA SAUSAGES, SLICED
THINLY

25 g (1 oz) BUTTER

1 TABLESPOON WORCESTERSHIRE SAUCE

AVOCADO AND CHEESE

1 MEDIUM-SIZE AVOCADO, CHOPPED ROUGHLY

125 g (4 oz) CREAM CHEESE

FRESHLY GROUND BLACK PEPPER

POOR MAN'S CAVIARE WITH SOURED CREAM

4 TEASPOONS BLACK OR RED LUMPFISH ROE

150 ml (¼ PINT) SOURED CREAM

1 TABLESPOON CHOPPED FRESH CHIVES

A SMALL PINCH OF CAYENNE PEPPER

Gratin dauphinoise

The vegetable equivalent of creamy rice
pudding!

SERVES 4–6

1 kg (2 lb) POTATOES, PREFERABLY DESIRÉE OR
EDWARDS

1 LARGE GARLIC CLOVE, HALVED, PLUS 1 SMALL
GARLIC CLOVE, CHOPPED VERY FINELY

25 g (1 oz) BUTTER

1 EGG

250 ml (8 fl oz) HOT MILK

250 ml (8 fl oz) DOUBLE CREAM

50 g (2 oz) GRUYÈRE CHEESE, GRATED

FRESHLY GRATED NUTMEG, SALT AND FRESHLY
GROUND BLACK PEPPER

Preheat and prepare the barbecue for
indirect heat cooking, following the
instructions on page 33.

Peel the potatoes and slice them very
thinly (a wooden mandoline is perfect for
this task). Plunge the potato slices into a
bowl of cold water and stir around to wash
off some of the starch. Drain and dry the
slices very thoroughly in a clean tea towel.

Rub the inside of an earthenware *gratin*
dish with the cut garlic and then grease with
the butter. Place the potato slices in layers,
sprinkling each layer with the finely chopped
garlic and nutmeg, salt and pepper to taste.

Whisk the egg, milk and cream
together, and pour the mixture over the
potato slices, ensuring the top layer is
completely covered. Cover the top with
the cheese.

Cook, with medium heat, for 1–1¼
hours or until the potatoes are tender when
pierced with a skewer.

Herb
and sesame
new potatoes
Page 107

Gem squash
à Nolan
Page 102

Spiced peaches
Page 114

Mixed fruit and bread kebabs
Page 115

Pizza
mozzarella with
tomato sauce
Page 122

Apple pie
Page 118

Potato and cheese casserole

SERVES 4–6

00 g (10 oz) CAN OF CONDENSED CREAM OF CHICKEN SOUP

150 ml (¼ PINT) MILK

125 g (4 oz) GRATED CHEDDAR CHEESE

4 MEDIUM-SIZE POTATOES, PEELED AND SLICED THINLY

2 TABLESPOONS FINELY CHOPPED ONION

1 TEASPOON SALT

GOOD PINCH OF FRESHLY GROUND BLACK PEPPER

1 TABLESPOON SOFT BUTTER OR MARGARINE

½ TEASPOON VERY FINELY CHOPPED FRESH PARSLEY

Preheat and prepare the barbecue for indirect heat cooking, following the instructions on page 33.

In a shallow casserole, mix the chicken soup and milk to a smooth cream. Stir in 0 g (2 oz) of the cheese, the potatoes, onion, salt and pepper. Dot with the butter or margarine and sprinkle over the remaining cheese and the parsley.

Cook, with medium heat, for about 1¼ hours or until the potatoes are tender.

Spicy nut roast

A delicious recipe that, although produced with the vegetarian barbecuer in mind, has equal taste appeal for the many members of the meat eating fraternity. It also tastes good cold, when it goes well with a salad.

SERVES 4

1 TABLESPOON OIL, PLUS EXTRA FOR GREASING

2 MEDIUM-SIZE ONIONS, CHOPPED FINELY

1 LARGE OR 2 SMALL GREEN PEPPERS, DE-SEEDED AND CHOPPED FINELY

50 g (2 oz) PECAN NUTS, CHOPPED FINELY

175 g (6 oz) WALNUT HALVES, CHOPPED FINELY

75 g (3 oz) FRESH BREADCRUMBS, PREFERABLY WHOLEMEAL

1 TEASPOON EACH CHOPPED FRESH THYME AND CHOPPED FRESH PARSLEY OR 1 TEASPOON DRIED MIXED HERBS

1 GARLIC CLOVE, CHOPPED VERY FINELY

1 TABLESPOON MILD CURRY POWDER OR 1 TEASPOON HOT CURRY POWDER

250 g (8 oz) FIRM RIPE TOMATOES, SKINNED AND CHOPPED

1 EGG, BEATEN

SALT AND FRESHLY GROUND BLACK PEPPER

Preheat and prepare the barbecue for indirect heat cooking, following the instructions on page 33.

Heat the oil, add the onions and pepper(s) and gently fry for about 10 minutes, or until they are soft.

Meanwhile, combine the nuts and breadcrumbs together in a large bowl. Add the herbs, garlic, curry powder and seasoning.

Stir the onion and pepper mixture, chopped tomatoes and beaten egg into the nut mixture. Bind all together.

Spoon the mixture into a greased 18 cm (7-inch) square cake tin or the equivalent in an ovenproof dish. Bake, with medium heat, for 30–45 minutes until golden brown.

Fruit & puddings

Most fruit can be cooked directly on the grill over a moderate heat but needs frequent basting with butter or a made-up basting sauce.

The alternative, apart from incorporating the fruit in a pie or crumble, is to wrap the prepared fruit, together with the basting juices, in a foil parcel.

Grilled grapefruit

A refreshing starter, entrée or dessert.

SERVES 6

3 GRAPEFRUIT

3 TABLESPOONS CLEAR HONEY OR BROWN SUGAR

3 TABLESPOONS SWEET SHERRY (OPTIONAL)

6 MARASCHINO CHERRIES

Preheat and prepare the barbecue for grilling or indirect heat cooking, following the instructions on page 30 or 33.

Slice each grapefruit in half, cut the segments loose and remove the pips.

Place each grapefruit half on a piece of doubled aluminium foil large enough to enclose the fruit. Spoon over about half a tablespoon of the honey or brown sugar, and half a tablespoon of the sherry, if using. Put a cherry in the centre of each half before wrapping the edges of the foil together securely.

Place the packages on the grill and cook, over medium heat, for approximately 15 minutes.

Alternatively, omit the cherries, leave the packages open, with the edges turned up to contain the juices, and cook by the indirect heat method for 15–20 minutes. (This method makes the sugar or honey caramelise.) Place the cherries on top when the cooking is completed.

Spiced peaches

Pictured on page 110
Spiced peaches are delicious served as a dessert with cream or yogurt; they also go well with ham, pork chops and poultry.

SERVES 4

4 RIPE, FIRM PEACHES

50 g (2 oz) SOFT BROWN SUGAR

1 TABLESPOON WORCESTERSHIRE SAUCE

A PINCH OF GROUND CINNAMON

A PINCH OF GROUND GINGER

Halve and stone the peaches.

Place the sugar, Worcestershire sauce, cinnamon and ginger in a saucepan and heat very gently until the sugar has dissolved. Arrange the peach halves in a shallow foil tray and spoon the sugar mixture over them. Leave the peaches for 2–3 hours, turning them occasionally.

Preheat and prepare the barbecue for grilling, following the instructions on page 30.

Lightly drain the peaches and grill, over medium heat, until they are heated through and beginning to brown.

Barbados oranges

As an alternative to rum I suggest you use the equivalent amount of kirsch liqueur.

SERVES 1

1 ORANGE, PREFERABLY SEEDLESS

1 TABLESPOON BROWN SUGAR

A PINCH OF GROUND CINNAMON

1 TABLESPOON RUM

1 TABLESPOON SOFT BUTTER OR MARGARINE

Preheat and prepare the barbecue for grilling, following the instructions on page 30.

Peel the orange, removing the pips if necessary, and carefully separate into segments. Place the segments on a piece of doubled aluminium foil. Sprinkle over the brown sugar, cinnamon and rum. Dot the segments with the butter or margarine before wrapping the edges of the foil together securely.

Place the package on the grill and cook, over medium heat, for 15–20 minutes.

Serve topped with whipped cream or vanilla ice cream.

Mixed fruit and bread kebabs

Pictured on page 110

A beautiful creation particularly appropriate for those 'special' barbecue occasions. Take my tip and make up an extra skewer or two consisting solely of bread cubes – they are very 'moreish' (extra butter and caster sugar will be required if you do so).

SERVES 6

2 RIPE, FIRM PEARS, PEELED AND CORED

MELON BALLS FROM 1 SMALL MELON

JUICE OF 2 LEMONS

2 ORANGES, CUT INTO 1 cm (½-INCH) SLICES

1 SMALL PINEAPPLE, PEELED AND CORED, OR 250 g
(8 oz) CAN OF PINEAPPLE CHUNKS

12 LARGE FIRM STRAWBERRIES

2 SMALL FIRM BANANAS, EACH CUT INTO 3

6 LARGE GRAPES, PREFERABLY SEEDLESS

125 g (4 oz) CASTER SUGAR, PLUS EXTRA FOR DUSTING

3 TABLESPOONS LIQUEUR

4 TABLESPOONS WHITE WINE

1 WHITE LOAF, CRUSTS REMOVED

125 g (4 oz) BUTTER, MELTED

OIL FOR GREASING

Cut the pears into large chunks. Place them, together with the melon balls and the lemon juice, in a large bowl. Quarter each orange slice and cut the fresh pineapple, if using, into 2.5 cm (1-inch) cubes.

Place the orange pieces, fresh or canned pineapple chunks, strawberries, bananas and grapes in the bowl and add half the sugar, the chosen liqueur and the white wine. Mix gently with your hands and leave the fruit to macerate in a cool place for 20–30 minutes.

Preheat and prepare the barbecue for grilling, following the instructions on page 30.

Slice the bread into 2.5 cm (1-inch) cubes and brush each, all over, with the melted butter. Toss the bread cubes in a bowl with the remaining sugar and coat them evenly.

Thread a selection of the fruit, together with two pieces of bread, on to long, oiled metal, preferably flat-bladed, skewers.

Grill over medium heat for about 5 minutes, turning and dusting with more sugar, until the kebabs are evenly browned and lightly caramelised.

If liked, warm the remaining marinade and sprinkle it over the kebabs before serving.

Cinnamon stuffed apples

If you are not too keen on cinnamon, try substituting 2 tablespoons of rum (or a little rum flavouring if the stuffed apples are for children).

SERVES 6

6 MEDIUM-SIZE COOKING APPLES, CORED

125 g (4 oz) BROWN SUGAR

2 TEASPOONS GROUND CINNAMON

A PINCH OF GROUND CLOVES

40 g (1½ oz) WALNUTS, CHOPPED FINELY

40 g (1½ oz) RAISINS, CHOPPED FINELY

1 TABLESPOON LEMON JUICE

6 TEASPOONS SOFT BUTTER

Preheat and prepare the barbecue for grilling, following the instructions on page 30.

Place each apple on a piece of doubled aluminium foil about 20 cm (8 inches) square. Combine the brown sugar, cinnamon, cloves, walnuts, raisins and lemon juice and use to fill the centres of the apples. Top each apple with a teaspoon of the butter. Bring the edges of the foil up to enclose the apples securely.

Grill the wrapped apples over medium heat for 40–50 minutes, or until the apples feel soft when pressed.

Serve topped with whipped cream or ice cream.

Pam and Ron's stuffed pears

An old favourite of mine, borrowed originally from the Heaths, who are great friends and great epicures.

SERVES 6

6 RIPE, FIRM COMICE PEARS, STALKS INTACT

JUICE OF 2 LEMONS

BUTTER FOR GREASING

CASTER SUGAR FOR DUSTING

STUFFING

50 g (2 oz) UNSALTED BUTTER

25 g (1 oz) CASTER SUGAR

25 g (1 oz) GROUND ALMONDS

GRATED ZEST OF 1 LEMON

25 g (1 oz) GLACÉ CHERRIES, CHOPPED FINELY

A PINCH OF GROUND CINNAMON

A PINCH OF GROUND GINGER

1 TEASPOON KIRSCH

For the stuffing, cream together the butter and sugar. Add the ground almonds, grated lemon zest, glacé cherries, cinnamon, ginger and kirsch and mix well.

Lightly trim the base of the pears so they stand upright. Thinly peel the pears, taking care to leave the stalks intact. Put the lemon juice in a saucer. Stand each pear in the saucer and brush liberally with the juice. Cut the top off each pear about 2.5 cm (1 inch) below the base of the stalk and reserve. Scoop out the cores, using a narrow, sharp-pointed teaspoon and leaving about 1 cm (½ inch) of the flesh at the base intact.

Preheat and prepare the barbecue for grilling or indirect heat cooking, following the instructions on page 30 or 33.

Stuff the pear cavities with the butter mixture. Replace the pear tops and stand

ach pear on a lightly greased 25 cm
(10-inch) square of heavy-duty aluminium
foil. Brush the remaining lemon juice over
the pears and dust with caster sugar. Gather
and twist the foil round the base of the stalks
to secure.

Stand the packaged pears in a shallow
baking tin or a double thickness foil drip pan
(see Tools and Accessories). Cook with
medium heat by the indirect heat method
for about 45 minutes, or for about 40
minutes by direct heat. The pears are ready
when they feel soft when gently squeezed –
take care not to overcook them. Handle the
pears by the stalks with a gloved hand.

Serve the pears with single cream,
if wished.

Rum chocolate banana split

A dish for cooks with a steady hand, time to
spare and, if increasing the quantity, sweet-
toothed guests – young or old.

SERVES 1

1 LARGE MEDIUM-RIPE, FIRM BANANA

½ LEMON

1 TEASPOON – 1 TABLESPOON RUM OR A FEW DROPS
OF RUM FLAVOURING

25 g (1 oz) DARK EATING CHOCOLATE, CHOPPED

2 MARSHMALLOWS, EACH CUT INTO 8

Peel the banana and place on the centre of a
piece of heavy-duty foil (or use a double
thickness of ordinary foil) about 23 × 15 cm
(9 × 6 inches) in size. Squeeze the juice from
the lemon over the banana.

Using a small-bladed knife, carefully
cut a wedge from the banana along its
length and reserve. The cavity should be
roughly 1 cm (½ inch) wide and 1 cm
(½ inch) deep.

Sprinkle the rum or rum flavouring
into the cavity. Partially fill the cavity with
the chocolate and top with the marshmallow
pieces. Press the banana wedge firmly back
into place. Lap the long edges of the foil
together, leaving a small air space. Firmly
squeeze the open ends of the package and
turn the crushed ends upwards so the
package is roughly boat-shaped. Chill the
package in the refrigerator until required,
keeping the 'boat' upright.

Preheat and prepare the barbecue for
grilling, following the instructions on
page 30.

Place the package on the grill and cook
over medium heat for about 10 minutes or
until the chocolate softens. If cooking lots of
bananas, check the progress of one of the
packages after 7 or 8 minutes; overcooking
makes the banana flesh pulpy and
unattractive.

Serve the banana with whipped cream
or vanilla ice cream.

Jersey Jean's banana delight

During one of my frequent visits to Jersey a
kind lady, who had witnessed my morning
barbecue demonstration, returned after
lunch bearing her own version of barbecued
spiced bananas. All those fortunate enough
to sample the cooked, sauce-enriched
bananas declared the taste delightful. I
particularly appreciated being able to see the
bananas during cooking, which is not
possible when following my standard foil-
wrapped, spiced banana recipe. With mine a
minute or so of accidental overcooking
results in the banana's girth expanding
before collapsing into a flat, pulpy mass –
a culinary crime I have too often been
guilty of!

SERVES 4

3 TABLESPOONS BANANA OR OTHER LIQUEUR

1 TABLESPOON BRANDY

2 TABLESPOONS SOFT BROWN SUGAR

4 LARGE MEDIUM-RIPE, FIRM BANANAS

Combine the liqueur, brandy and brown sugar and mix well.

Peel the bananas, cut in half lengthways and arrange them in a shallow foil tray. Spoon the sugar mixture over the bananas, cover and leave for about 30 minutes, turning the bananas over once or twice.

Preheat and prepare the barbecue for grilling, following the instructions on page 30.

Centre the tray on the grill and cook, over low to medium heat, for about 8–10 minutes until the bananas are barely tender, carefully turning them over roughly half-way through cooking.

Serve hot with the sauce and with whipped cream or ice cream, if wished.

Apple pie

Pictured on page 111
I can happily confirm that the pie shown on page 111 tasted as scrumptious as it looks!

SERVES ABOUT 6

SHORTCRUST PASTRY

250 g (8 oz) PLAIN FLOUR, PLUS EXTRA FOR ROLLING

A PINCH OF SALT

125 g (4 oz) BUTTER OR MARGARINE, CUT INTO SMALL PIECES

2–3 TABLESPOONS COLD WATER

MILK FOR BRUSHING

CASTER SUGAR FOR SPRINKLING

FILLING

500 g (1 lb) BRAMLEY COOKING APPLES AND/OR COX'S ORANGE PIPPIN DESSERT APPLES, PEELED, CORED AND SLICED THINLY

125 g (4 oz) BROWN OR WHITE SUGAR

GRATED ZEST OF ½ LEMON

1–2 CLOVES (OPTIONAL)

To make the pastry, sift the flour and salt into a large mixing bowl, add the butter or margarine and rub in until the mixture resembles fine breadcrumbs. Mix in enough cold water with a round-bladed or palette knife to make a stiff dough. Lightly press the pastry into a ball and leave, wrapped in foil or polythene, in the refrigerator for 30 minutes.

Divide the pastry into two pieces. Roll out one half on a floured surface to a circle large enough to cover an ovenproof plate. Carefully lift the dough on to the plate. Pile the sliced apples on top and sprinkle over the sugar, lemon zest and cloves, if using. Dampen the edge of the dough with a little cold water. Roll out the remaining dough and carefully lay it over the apples. Press the edges together to seal and trim them with a sharp knife. Flute the edges.

Preheat and prepare the barbecue for indirect heat cooking, following the instructions on page 33.

Brush the pastry with milk and lightly dust with caster sugar. Make a small slit in the top of the pie to allow the steam to escape.

Reduce the heat to medium (200°C/400°F). Bake the pie for 15 minutes and then reduce the temperature slightly (to about 180°C/350°F) and bake for a further 25 minutes or until the pastry is nicely browned. To test whether the pie is cooked use a thin metal skewer to pierce, remove and check a piece of apple from below the steam slit.

Remove the pie from the barbecue, sprinkle lightly with more caster sugar and serve.

Barbecued bread and butter pudding

I adore Bread and Butter Pudding and regard it as the quintessential British pud. As far as 'calorie counters' are concerned, the following recipe is 'naughty but nice'!

SERVES 4

BUTTER FOR SPREADING AND GREASING

8 THIN SLICES OF BREAD CUT FROM A SMALL LOAF

15 g (½ oz) CANDIED LEMON OR ORANGE PEEL, CHOPPED FINELY

75 g (3 oz) CURRANTS

300 ml (½ PINT) MILK

75 ml (3 fl oz) DOUBLE CREAM

50 g (2 oz) CASTER SUGAR

¼ TEASPOON GRATED LEMON ZEST

3 EGGS, BEATEN

A LITTLE FRESHLY GRATED NUTMEG

Butter the bread. Butter a 1-litre (1¾-pint) oblong baking dish.

Arrange one layer of buttered bread over the base of the dish. Sprinkle the candied peel and half the currants over the bread and cover with another layer of bread and the remaining currants.

Combine the milk and cream and stir in the sugar and lemon zest. Whisk the beaten eggs into the mixture and pour over the bread. Sprinkle over a little nutmeg and leave to stand for 30 minutes.

Preheat and prepare the barbecue for indirect heat cooking, following the instructions on page 33.

Place the dish in the centre of the grill and adjust the control knob to a position between low and medium (180°C/350°F). Bake for 30–40 minutes or until the pudding is set and the top golden and crisp.

Aran rice pudding

A deliciously rich rice pudding – the skin caramelises hiding a creamy, gooey middle.

SERVES 4–6

125 g (4 oz) SHORT-GRAIN RICE, WASHED AND DRAINED

900 ml (1½ PINTS) MILK OR A MIXTURE OF HALF WATER AND HALF EVAPORATED MILK

50 g (2 oz) BUTTER, PLUS EXTRA FOR GREASING

50 g (2 oz) CASTER SUGAR

2 EGGS

GRATED ZEST OF ½ LEMON

FRESHLY GRATED NUTMEG

Put the rice into a heavy based saucepan, add the milk or water and evaporated milk and bring slowly to just below simmering. Allow the rice to cook on very gently for about 10 minutes or until the rice is barely tender.

Add the butter and sugar and stir until they have completely dissolved. Remove the saucepan from the heat and allow the contents to cool for 2–3 minutes.

Butter a 1-litre (1¾-pint) ovenproof pie dish. Preheat and prepare the barbecue for indirect heat cooking, following the instructions on page 33.

Beat the eggs and lemon zest together and stir into the rice mixture. Pour the mixture into the pie dish and sprinkle the surface with grated nutmeg.

Bake, with low to medium heat, for about 35–40 minutes (adding a few more minutes to the cooking time may give the pudding a thicker, creamier consistency, but over-cooking and/or using too high heat may turn the pudding into a rice short-cake!)

Bread & pizzas

There are few things in the world of food that provide more satisfaction than the smell and taste of home-baked bread. Why not, therefore, use your gas barbecue occasionally as an *al fresco* baker's oven?

Daily bread

Pictured on page 112

Having tried your hand at baking a standard loaf, there is nothing to stop you tackling the more fancy shapes such as cottage, cob, bloomer or plait; or indeed, using your yeast dough to bake the odd batch of sticky buns or light brioches. White and brown packet bread mixes are readily available should you wish to cut a few corners.

MAKES 2 LOAVES

1 kg (2 lb) PLAIN FLOUR, PLUS EXTRA FOR KNEADING

2 TEASPOONS SALT

15–20 g (½–¾ oz) FRESH YEAST OR 10–15 g (¼–½ oz) DRIED YEAST

½ TEASPOON SUGAR

600 ml (1 PINT) LUKEWARM WATER

LARD FOR GREASING

Sift the flour and salt into a warm mixing bowl. If using fresh yeast, cream it with the sugar and then add the mixture to the water. If using dried yeast, add it with the sugar to the water.

Make a well in the centre of the flour mixture and pour in the liquid. Draw in enough flour to make a thick batter. Sprinkle the batter with more of the flour. Cover the bowl with a damp cloth and leave in a warm place for 15–20 minutes or until bubbles break through the floury surface.

Work the batter into a spongy dough and turn it out on to a floured surface.

Knead well until the dough is no longer sticky, dusting the dough occasionally with flour. Place the dough in a bowl greased with lard.

Turn over the dough and make a shallow cross-cut on the top. Cover the bowl with a damp cloth and leave, in a warm draught-free place, for 1–1½ hours until the dough has doubled in bulk.

Grease two 23 × 13 × 7.5 cm (9- × 5- × 3-inch) loaf tins.

Turn the dough out on to a floured surface and knead lightly for a minute. Cut the dough in half and make a loaf shape with each. Place in the prepared tins. Stand the tins on a baking sheet, cover with the cloth and prove in a warm place for 10–15 minutes or until the dough begins to swell.

Preheat and prepare the barbecue for indirect heat cooking, following the instructions on page 33. Adjust the control knob to a position between medium and high just before baking.

Place the proved loaves on the barbecue and bake for about 20 minutes. Reduce the heat to medium (200°C/400°F) and continue baking for 15–20 minutes until the loaves are well browned and shrinking slightly from the sides of the tin.

Tip the finished loaves out on to a rack to cool, checking that they are cooked by tapping the bottoms to see if they sound hollow. A skewer may be inserted into the centre to see if it comes out clean as a double check.

Wholemeal rolls

MAKES 12 ROLLS

1 TEASPOON BROWN SUGAR

250 ml (8 fl oz) LUKEWARM WATER

25 g (1 oz) FRESH YEAST OR 15 g (½ oz) DRIED YEAST

500 g (1 lb) WHOLEMEAL FLOUR, PLUS EXTRA FOR
KNEADING AND DUSTING

1 TEASPOON SALT

50 g (2 oz) CRACKED WHEAT

Dissolve the sugar in a third of the lukewarm water and add the fresh or dried yeast. Mix well and leave until foamy in a warm place.

Mix the flour and salt in a large bowl. Stir the yeast mixture into the flour, gradually add the remaining water and mix with your hands to make a smooth dough. Knead the dough on a floured surface for about 5 minutes until it is elastic and no longer sticky.

Divide the dough into 12 pieces and shape into rolls. Place, spaced apart, on a floured baking sheet and leave to rise covered with a damp tea towel. Leave in a warm place for 1–1½ hours or until nearly doubled in size.

Preheat and prepare the barbecue for indirect heat cooking, following the instructions on page 33. Adjust the control knob to a position between medium and high just before placing the rolls on the grill.

Sprinkle the rolls with the cracked wheat and place the sheet on the barbecue. Bake for 10–15 minutes.

Cheese and herb rolls

Pictured on page 112

MAKES 8

175 g (6 oz) BUTTER, SOFTENED

125 g (4 oz) BLUE CHEESE OR GRATED CHEDDAR
CHEESE

1 TABLESPOON FINELY CHOPPED ONION

1½ TABLESPOONS CHOPPED FRESH PARSLEY

1 TEASPOON CRUSHED FRESH ROSEMARY

1 TEASPOON DRIED BASIL

8 BREAD ROLLS, HALVED

Preheat and prepare the barbecue for grilling, following the instructions on page 30.

Cream together the butter and cheese and stir in the onion, parsley, rosemary and basil. Spread the mixture over the cut sides of each roll. Place the halves together and wrap each roll in aluminium foil.

Place the rolls on the grill and heat through over medium to high heat for 12–15 minutes, turning once.

Pizza dough

Your gas barbecue may not bear much resemblance to a pizzeria in a small Italian village, but the end result – smell, taste and bubbling surface – is not that far removed from the genuine article. This recipe will provide a quickly made base for whatever topping your cupboard and imagination can provide. The dough should be sufficient for two pizzas, each serving two to four.

MAKES 2 PIZZA BASES

15 g (½ oz) DRIED YEAST

75–125 ml (3–4 fl oz) LUKEWARM WATER

250 g (8 oz) STRONG WHITE FLOUR OR WHOLEMEAL
FLOUR, PLUS EXTRA FOR KNEADING

1 TEASPOON SALT

1 EGG, BEATEN

1 TEASPOON OIL

Mix the yeast with the water in a cup and stand it in a warm place for 10 minutes or until frothy.

Sift the flour and salt together in a mixing bowl. Pour in the yeast mixture and the beaten egg and mix, using one hand, to a scone-like dough that leaves the bowl clean, adding an extra drop or two of warm water if necessary.

Transfer the dough on to a floured work surface and knead for about 10 minutes until it is smooth and elastic. Return the dough to the bowl and rub the surface with the oil. Cover the dough with a clean, damp cloth and leave in a warmish place for about an hour, or until it has doubled in size.

Knead the dough lightly for a few minutes. It is now ready to shape into pizzas.

Pizza mozzarella with tomato sauce

Pictured on page 111

SERVES 2–4

½ QUANTITY OF PIZZA DOUGH (ABOVE)

TOMATO SAUCE

2 TABLESPOONS OIL

1 MEDIUM-SIZE SPANISH ONION, CHOPPED FINELY

2 GARLIC CLOVES, CRUSHED

2 × 425 g (14 oz) CAN OF ITALIAN TOMATOES

½ TEASPOON DRIED BASIL

1 BAY LEAF

SALT AND FRESHLY GROUND BLACK PEPPER

TOPPING

2 TABLESPOONS OIL

125 g (4 oz) MOZZARELLA CHEESE, SLICED THINLY

50 g (2 oz) CAN OF ANCHOVY FILLETS, DRAINED AND CHOPPED

10 LARGE BLACK OLIVES, STONED AND HALVED

1 TEASPOON DRIED OREGANO

1 TABLESPOON GRATED PARMESAN CHEESE

To make the sauce, heat the oil in a saucepan and fry the onion until soft and golden. Add the garlic, tomatoes, basil, bay leaf and salt and pepper to taste. Simmer over gentle heat for about 40 minutes or until the tomato mixture is thick. Remove the pan from the heat, discard the bay leaf and leave the sauce to cool.

Place the pizza dough in either one large, shallow pizza tin about 25 cm (10 inches) square, or two small tins. The dough should line the bottom and sides of the tin.

Brush the dough with a little of the oil. Cover it with the tomato sauce and lay the cheese over the surface. Arrange the anchovies and olives attractively and sprinkle over the oregano and parmesan. Trickle the remaining oil over the top. Leave the pizza(s) for 15 minutes before baking.

Preheat and prepare the barbecue for indirect heat cooking, following the instructions on page 33.

Place the pizza(s) on the grill and adjust the control knob to a position between medium and high (220°C/425°F). Bake the pizza(s) for 15–20 minutes. To check that the dough base is fully baked, lift an edge with a fish slice and take a look.

Serve the pizza(s) straight from the barbecue, or cool on a wire rack to make this a delicious cold addition to a picnic meal.

VARIATION

SALAMI AND MUSHROOM TOPPING

125 g (4 oz) SALAMI OR GARLIC SAUSAGE, CUT INTO MATCHSTICKS

75 g (3 oz) MUSHROOMS, SLICED THINLY

75 g (3 oz) TOMATOES, SLICED THINLY

75 g (3 oz) MOZZARELLA OR BEL PAESE CHEESE, SLICED THINLY

SALT AND FRESHLY GROUND BLACK PEPPER

Layer the salami or garlic sausage, mushrooms and tomatoes on top of the tomato sauce. Season with salt and pepper and cover with the cheese slices.

Salads

Tomato and onion salad

A tasty and refreshing starter, especially when served with some crusty french bread.

SERVES 4

4 LARGE OR 6 SMALL FIRM, RIPE TOMATOES, SKINNED AND SLICED THINLY

2 MEDIUM-SIZE ONIONS, SLICED THINLY AND SEPARATED INTO RINGS

1 TEASPOON CHOPPED FRESH BASIL OR ½ TEASPOON DRIED BASIL

2 TABLESPOONS CHOPPED FRESH PARSLEY

1 QUANTITY OF VINAIGRETTE DRESSING (PAGE 125)

Arrange the tomato slices on a large flat plate – try not to over-lap the slices if you prepare the salad more than an hour before it is eaten because it tends to make the slices soggy. Scatter the onion rings over the tomatoes.

Sprinkle with the chopped herbs and pour over the dressing.

Brown rice and vegetable salad

SERVES 6–8

1 TABLESPOON GROUNDNUT OIL

300 g (10 oz) BROWN RICE

600 ml (1 PINT) BOILING WATER

4 TABLESPOONS VINAIGRETTE DRESSING (PAGE 125)

2 LARGE TOMATOES, CUT INTO THIN WEDGES

½ RED OR GREEN PEPPER, DE-SEEDED AND CHOPPED FINELY

5 cm (2-INCH) PIECE OF CUCUMBER, CHOPPED FINELY

1 MEDIUM-SIZE RED DESSERT APPLE, CORED AND CHOPPED

1 SMALL CELERY STICK, CHOPPED FINELY

2 TABLESPOONS FINELY CHOPPED SPRING ONION OR ONION

25 g (1 oz) WALNUTS, CHOPPED FINELY

25 g (1 oz) CURRANTS

SALT AND FRESHLY GROUND BLACK PEPPER

Heat the oil in a saucepan, add the rice and stir to coat all the grains. Add about 1 teaspoon of salt, pour over the boiling water and bring back to the boil. Stir once only, cover and simmer gently for 40 minutes or until all the liquid has been absorbed and the rice is tender.

Empty the rice into a salad bowl and fluff it with a fork. Pour the prepared dressing over whilst the rice is still warm. Cool.

When the rice is cold, stir in all the other ingredients, adding a little more dressing if desired, and season to taste. Keep the salad in a cool place until required.

Bean sprout salad with koi-kuchi-shoyu dressing

A colourful and delicious salad. ('Koi-Kuchi-Shoyu' is the Japanese phrase for 'regular soy sauce'.)

SERVES 4

125 g (4 oz) CARROT, CUT INTO MATCHSTICKS

250 g (8 oz) BEAN SPROUTS

2 SMALL GREEN PEPPERS, QUARTERED, DE-SEEDED AND CUT INTO MATCHSTICKS

1 SMALL RED PEPPER, QUARTERED, DE-SEEDED AND CUT INTO MATCHSTICKS

2 TEASPOONS SESAME SEEDS, TOASTED (OPTIONAL)

SALT

DRESSING

3 TABLESPOONS SOY SAUCE

1 TABLESPOON OLIVE OR GROUNDNUT OIL

2 TABLESPOONS RED WINE VINEGAR

1 TABLESPOON SESAME OIL

First make the dressing by shaking all the ingredients together in a screw-top jar.

Bring 300 ml (½ pint) of water to the boil. Add ¼ teaspoon of salt and the carrot strips and blanch for 1 minute. Add the bean sprouts and peppers and, when the water simmers again, remove the pan from the heat. Drain off the water through a colander, compress the vegetables lightly to remove excess water and fan vigorously for 2–3 minutes to cool quickly.

Tip the salad into a large bowl, add the dressing and mix it all together gently.

Serve the salad in small individual bowls and sprinkle with the sesame seeds, if using.

Oriental cucumber and radish salad

SERVES 4

12 FAT RADISHES

1 SMALL CUCUMBER

DRESSING

1½ TABLESPOONS SOY SAUCE

½ TABLESPOON RED WINE VINEGAR

2 TEASPOONS SESAME OIL

½ TEASPOON SUGAR

Cut the tops off the radishes. Crush each radish (use the side of a broad-bladed knife, or cleaver, for this task) to open it up whilst keeping it intact.

Cut the cucumber into pieces approximately 5 cm (2 inches) long and crush. Cut the crushed cucumber lengthways into halves or quarters.

Combine all the ingredients for the dressing and mix well.

Arrange the radishes and cucumber pieces on a plate, pour over the dressing and serve.

Salade Niçoise

SERVES 4–6

1 FIRM ROUND LETTUCE

3 FIRM TOMATOES, SKINNED, DE-SEEDED AND
QUARTERED

½ SMALL CUCUMBER, PEELED AND CUT INTO SMALL
CHUNKS

1 MEDIUM-SIZE RED PEPPER, DE-SEEDED AND CUT
INTO NARROW STRIPS

2 SPRING ONIONS, CHOPPED FINELY

125 g (4 oz) FRENCH BEANS, COOKED

2 HARD-BOILED EGGS, QUARTERED

50 g (2 oz) BLACK OLIVES

200 g (7 oz) CAN OF TUNA FISH, DRAINED WELL AND
BROKEN INTO CHUNKS

6 ANCHOVY FILLETS, HALVED LENGTHWAYS

2 TEASPOONS CAPERS (OPTIONAL)

VINAIGRETTE DRESSING

1 GARLIC CLOVE, CRUSHED

1 TEASPOON SALT

1 TEASPOON MUSTARD POWDER

1 TABLESPOON RED OR WHITE WINE VINEGAR

A PINCH OF FRESHLY GROUND BLACK PEPPER

6 TABLESPOONS GOOD QUALITY GREEN OLIVE OIL

1 TABLESPOON CHOPPED FRESH TARRAGON
(OPTIONAL)

First make the dressing. Using a pestle and mortar, pound the garlic with the salt until you have a smooth paste. Add the mustard powder, vinegar and pepper and mix thoroughly until the salt has completely dissolved. Add the olive oil and tarragon, if using. Pour the vinaigrette into a screw-top jar and, just before dressing the salad, give it a good shake to blend all the ingredients thoroughly.

Shake the lettuce dry. Remove the outer leaves and arrange around the base of a large salad bowl. Cut the heart into quarters and place on the base of the bowl. Sprinkle over a little of the dressing.

Arrange the tomato and cucumber pieces in layers over the lettuce with a little more dressing; then add the pepper strips, spring onions, and french beans. Top with the hard-boiled eggs, black olives and tuna fish.

Decorate the salad with the strips of anchovy fillet and the capers, if using. Spoon over more of the dressing and serve.

Caesar salad

Sometimes described as the classic American salad, this goes well with most barbecued food.

SERVES 4

3 TABLESPOONS LEMON JUICE

2 TABLESPOONS OLIVE OIL

2 TABLESPOONS RED WINE VINEGAR

1 TABLESPOON WORCESTERSHIRE SAUCE

4 GARLIC CLOVES, CRUSHED

6 SLICES OF WHITE BREAD, CRUSTS REMOVED, CUT
INTO 1 cm (½-INCH) CUBES

50 g (2 oz) BUTTER

1 COS LETTUCE

1 EGG, BEATEN WELL OR PARBOILED IN ITS SHELL
FOR 2 MINUTES

50 g (2 oz) ROQUEFORT OR BLUE CHEESE, CRUMBLED

50 g (2 oz) CAN OF ANCHOVY FILLETS, CUT
LENGTHWAYS INTO STRIPS (OPTIONAL)

SALT AND FRESHLY GROUND BLACK PEPPER

In a jug mix together the lemon juice, olive oil, vinegar, Worcestershire sauce and half the crushed garlic. Allow to stand for 4–6 hours. Strain to remove the garlic.

Toast the bread cubes on a baking sheet in a preheated moderately hot oven or on a preheated barbecue, stirring them occasionally until the cubes are lightly browned on all sides. Melt the butter in a large frying pan, add the remaining garlic and the toasted bread cubes and stir continuously until the cubes have absorbed the butter and are golden.

Separate the lettuce leaves, tearing the largest ones in half with your hands. Place the leaves in a large salad bowl. Pour the beaten or parboiled egg over the lettuce and add the dressing. Toss well until all traces of the egg disappear.

Add the crumbled cheese, anchovy fillets, if using, and bread cubes. Season to taste with salt and pepper and toss again.

Potato salad

SERVES 4–6

1 kg (2 lb) WAXY POTATOES WITH THEIR SKINS ON

½ TEASPOON MUSTARD POWDER

4 SPRING ONIONS, CHOPPED FINELY

150 ml (¼ PINT) MAYONNAISE (OPPOSITE)

2 TABLESPOONS CHOPPED FRESH PARSLEY

PAPRIKA FOR SPRINKLING

SALT AND FRESHLY GROUND BLACK PEPPER

Boil or steam the potatoes in their skins until just tender. Drain, peel and dice them.

Mix the mustard and spring onions into the mayonnaise and add salt and pepper to taste.

Add the mayonnaise to the potato and mix gently with a spoon until it is well coated – this process is easier if the potatoes are still warm. Taste and adjust the seasoning if necessary. Sprinkle with the chopped parsley and a little paprika.

Mayonnaise

It is essential that the oil, egg yolk and wine vinegar are at normal (cool rather than warm) room temperature.

MAKES ABOUT 150 ml (¼ PINT)

1 EGG YOLK

¼ TEASPOON SALT

½ TEASPOON MUSTARD POWDER

A PINCH OF FRESHLY GROUND WHITE PEPPER

150 ml (¼ PINT) OLIVE OR VEGETABLE OIL

1 TABLESPOON WHITE WINE VINEGAR OR LEMON JUICE

Place the egg yolk in a bowl and gradually beat in the salt, mustard and pepper. A wire balloon whisk is probably the best tool for this job; or use a small hand mixer or wooden spoon.

Add the oil, *drop by drop*, whisking vigorously after each addition. Once the mixture forms a shiny emulsion and has become thick (roughly half the oil will have been used), the oil can be added more quickly, say, 1 tablespoon at a time.

When the mixture is very thick, add the wine vinegar or lemon juice and mix in. Then blend in the remaining oil. The finished consistency should be similar to lightly whipped double cream. Taste and adjust the seasoning.

The mayonnaise can be stored in the refrigerator, in a covered container, for up to 2 weeks.

Note: if you prefer to use a blender to make the mayonnaise, use a whole egg and add the oil in a thin stream with the blender set at a moderate speed.

Drinks

Al fresco summertime drinks generally take the refreshing form of fruit cups and punches. Apart from being visually attractive and thirst quenching, cups and punches are generally low on stimulants and relatively inexpensive. A few recipes for fruit cups and punches are given but, as with barbecue sauces and marinades, I believe that making up one's own recipes is far more satisfying. Mix them up beforehand and keep in bottles or plastic containers in a cold box, with lots of ice cubes.

What wine is best to serve and drink is a matter of personal taste. Although white wines seem the obvious choice for *al fresco* summer parties, there are several red wines that take kindly, indeed benefit, from being served lightly chilled or even downright cool. However, in my opinion it would be a sad waste of really good wine to drink it in the great outdoors. The finest nose would probably experience great difficulty in capturing a fine wine's frail bouquet when competing with the garden's natural aromas. Add the tangy pungent smells emanating from a barbecue in full cry and the battle would be truly lost.

Wines which suit being drunk in the open air are those with pronounced fruity overtones and a really fresh acidity. Alsace, German Rieslings, and English wines feature in this category, and Gewürztraminers are excellent with spicy barbecue fare.

Should you need further help on what wine to buy for your next barbecue cook-out, ask your local off-licence manager. Another useful source of information is the descriptive label used by most shops and supermarkets outlining a wine's characteristics.

Sangrìa

SERVES 12

2 × 1 LITRE (1¾ PINTS) BOTTLE OF RED WINE
1 LITRE (1¾ PINTS) BOTTLE OF LEMONADE
4 TABLESPOONS BRANDY
2 TABLESPOONS CASTER SUGAR
1 LARGE ORANGE, CUT INTO THIN SLICES
1 LARGE LEMON, CUT INTO THIN SLICES
1 LARGE EATING APPLE, CORED AND CUT INTO THIN SLICES
ICE CUBES AND SODA WATER TO SERVE

Pour the red wine, lemonade and brandy into a large jug. Add the caster sugar, orange, lemon and apple. Leave to macerate and chill in a refrigerator for 2–3 hours.

When ready to serve, add a tray of ice cubes and soda water to taste.

Kir

This makes a refreshing and elegant aperitif with which to welcome guests at a party.

To make, simply stir one tablespoon of cassis (blackcurrant liqueur) or raspberry or blackcurrant syrup into every glass of well-chilled white wine.

Summer cider cup

SERVES 8

1 TRAY OF ICE CUBES
GRATED ZEST OF 2 LEMONS
1.2 LITRES (2 PINTS) CIDER
600 ml (1 PINT) SODA WATER
1 TABLESPOON BRANDY
1 TABLESPOON CURAÇAO
1 TABLESPOON KIRSCH

Place the ice cubes in a large jug. Add all the remaining ingredients, mix well and serve immediately.

Fruit punch

SERVES 8

250 g (8 oz) SUGAR

300 ml (½ PINT) WATER

300 ml (½ PINT) ORANGE JUICE, CHILLED

300 ml (½ PINT) PINEAPPLE JUICE, CHILLED

600 ml (1 PINT) COLD WEAK TEA

2 TABLESPOONS LEMON JUICE

300 ml (½ PINT) GINGER ALE, CHILLED

SLICED FRUIT IN SEASON, e.g. 1 APPLE, 1 ORANGE, 1
LEMON AND/OR 1 PASSION-FRUIT AND ½ PINEAPPLE

SPRIGS OF FRESH MINT

6 STRAWBERRIES, HALVED

CRUSHED ICE

Place the sugar and water in a saucepan and
stir over low heat until the sugar has
dissolved. Boil for 2–3 minutes. Cool and
add the fruit juices, cold tea and lemon juice.
Chill well.

Just before serving, add the ginger ale,
sliced fruit, mint sprigs, the strawberries and
crushed ice. Serve in chilled glasses
decorated with more mint sprigs.

Accompaniments

The prime function of a marinade is to
tenderise and enhance the flavour of cuts of
meat that may be lacking both. Sensibly
used, a marinade can promote a 'fourth
division' cut of meat into a 'second division'
one. There is, however, no substitute for
prime quality, so whenever possible buy
meat of the highest quality (not necessarily
of the highest price) to ensure good results.

The acid in a marinade, be it lemon
juice, wine vinegar, wine or pineapple juice,
acts as a tenderising agent; the fat (butter,
oil or margarine) gives moistness to very
lean meat and helps to protect the meat from
losing too much succulence when cooked
over high heat.

Some foods can be left to marinate in
the refrigerator for over 24 hours, while
others prefer to be briefly 'kissed' by the
marinade – for, say, 15–20 minutes –
before cooking.

If the marinade is acid, it is advisable to
use a glass or china receptacle. If the meat is
not fully covered by the marinade, it is
necessary to turn it occasionally. A good
way to turn food without fuss, is to place
both marinade and meat in a strong plastic
bag (or two just to be safe) which is tightly
sealed. As an extra safeguard, place the bag
in a baking tin.

If marinating the food overnight in the
refrigerator, remember to remove the meat
at least an hour before cooking. The drained
meat should be at room temperature before
being barbecued.

The distinction between marinades and
sauces can be hazy, but generally a marinade
is something applied to the food before
cooking, and a sauce is something that is
applied during cooking and then eaten as
part of the dish. Many marinades are better

heated before being brushed or spooned over the barbecuing food.

Sauces are best prepared in heavy-based saucepans and stirred with a wooden spoon. They can, of course, be pre-cooked in the kitchen, but a twin burner gas barbecue, especially one incorporating a fairly wide warming grill, is ideal for preparing and holding the sauce next to the grill on which the food is being cooked.

Most sauces, and certainly those containing sugar and/or tomato, are best brushed on to the meat during the final ten minutes or so of cooking in order to avoid the surface becoming burnt and over-flavoured.

A new, good quality, natural bristled paint brush, between 2.5–5 cm (1–2 inches) wide, is excellent for basting but, as it is short-handled, you will need to wear an oven glove or, preferably, a gauntlet. Thin sauces and marinades can be brushed on to food with a neatly tied bundle of herbs – very atmospheric!

Honey mint marinade

MAKES ABOUT 300 ml (½ PINT)

150 ml (¼ PINT) DRY WHITE WINE

4 TABLESPOONS CLEAR HONEY

1 TEASPOON SOY SAUCE

1 TABLESPOON CHOPPED FRESH MINT

1 TABLESPOON RED OR WHITE WINE VINEGAR

1 GARLIC CLOVE, CRUSHED

1 TEASPOON SALT

Combine all the ingredients and mix until well blended. Allow to stand for at least an hour before use.

Particularly suitable with lamb, but can be used for chicken. Allow the meat to marinate for 1–2 hours.

Soy-lemon marinade

MAKES ABOUT 300 ml (½ PINT)

6 TABLESPOONS LEMON JUICE

6 TABLESPOONS SOY SAUCE

4 TABLESPOONS GROUNDNUT OR SUNFLOWER OIL

1 TEASPOON SESAME OIL

½ TEASPOON FRESHLY GROUND BLACK PEPPER

1 GARLIC CLOVE, CRUSHED

1 BAY LEAF

Combine all the ingredients and allow the mixture to stand for at least an hour before use.

Excellent for joints of beef which can be left in the marinade – a strong well-sealed plastic bag is ideal for holding both joint and marinade – for up to three days in the refrigerator. The meat should be turned frequently and then drained well before roasting.

Soy sake marinade

MAKES ABOUT 300 ml (½ PINT)

4 TABLESPOONS SOY SAUCE

4 TABLESPOONS SAKE OR DRY SHERRY

3 TABLESPOONS GROUNDNUT OR SUNFLOWER OIL

2 TABLESPOONS CLEAR HONEY

1 TEASPOON FRESHLY GRATED ROOT GINGER OR A GOOD PINCH OF GROUND GINGER

1 GARLIC CLOVE, SLICED THINLY

Combine all the ingredients and mix well.

Use with red and white meats and fish.

Marinade vin rouge

MAKES ABOUT 450 ml (¾ PINT)

300 ml (½ PINT) DRY RED WINE

6 TABLESPOONS GROUNDNUT OR SUNFLOWER OIL

50 g (2 oz) FINELY CHOPPED SPRING ONION

2 GARLIC CLOVES, CRUSHED

1 TEASPOON DRIED WHOLE BASIL OR OREGANO

1 TEASPOON SALT

½ TEASPOON FRESHLY GROUND BLACK PEPPER

Combine all the ingredients in a heavy-based saucepan and heat until the marinade starts to simmer. Remove from the heat immediately, cover the pan and leave for about 1 hour to cool.

Use with beef or pork.

Wine, oil and dill marinade

MAKES ABOUT 150 ml (¼ PINT)

150 ml (¼ PINT) DRY WHITE WINE

3 TABLESPOONS OIL

1 TEASPOON PAPRIKA

½ TEASPOON SALT

1 TEASPOON SUGAR

A FEW SPRIGS OF FRESH DILL

4 FRESH CHIVE BLADES, CHOPPED

1 TABLESPOON VERY FINELY CHOPPED FRESH PARSLEY

A PINCH OF FRESHLY GROUND BLACK PEPPER

Combine all the ingredients and mix well. This is particularly suitable for fish. Pour over seafood and leave, covered and in a cool place, for about an hour before cooking.

Korean sesame marinade

MAKES ABOUT 300 ml (½ PINT)

150 ml (¼ PINT) SOY SAUCE

3 TABLESPOONS GROUNDNUT OIL

2 TEASPOONS SESAME OIL

1 TABLESPOON RED OR WHITE WINE VINEGAR

2 GARLIC CLOVES, CHOPPED VERY FINELY

2 TABLESPOONS SESAME SEEDS, TOASTED AND CRUSHED

A PINCH OF CAYENNE PEPPER

Combine all the ingredients and mix well. Use with pork, chicken or fish.

Teriyaki marinade

MAKES ABOUT 150 ml (¼ PINT)

1½ TABLESPOONS CLEAR HONEY

1½ TABLESPOONS GROUNDNUT OR SUNFLOWER OIL

4 TABLESPOONS SOY SAUCE

1 TABLESPOON DRY RED WINE OR RED WINE VINEGAR

1 TEASPOON FRESHLY GRATED ROOT GINGER OR A GOOD PINCH OF GROUND GINGER

1 LARGE GARLIC CLOVE, CRUSHED

Combine all the ingredients and mix well.

Use to marinate chicken, beef, spare ribs or fish. Meat will need to be marinated for 4–8 hours or overnight in the refrigerator – turn it occasionally. Fish only requires marinating for about 2–4 hours in the refrigerator. This also makes a superb basting sauce.

Sweet and sour barbecue sauce

MAKES ABOUT 300 ml (½ PINT)

250 ml (8 fl oz) TOMATO KETCHUP

150 ml (¼ PINT) ORANGE MARMALADE OR APRICOT JAM

2 TABLESPOONS LEMON JUICE

1 TEASPOON WORCESTERSHIRE SAUCE

1 TEASPOON SOY SAUCE

½ TEASPOON HORSERADISH SAUCE

½ TEASPOON SALT

A PINCH OF FRESHLY GROUND BLACK PEPPER

Put all the ingredients in a heavy-based saucepan and heat until simmering.

Serve with pork.

Jim's new universal sauce

This makes enough to reserve some for future home 'cook-outs' or to take in lieu of a bottle of wine to an away fixture.

MAKES ABOUT 1.2 LITRES (2 PINTS)

2 TABLESPOONS GROUNDNUT OIL

2 GARLIC CLOVES, CRUSHED

2 SMALL GREEN PEPPERS, DE-SEEDED AND CHOPPED FINELY

2 SMALL ONIONS, CHOPPED FINELY

125 g (4 oz) CELERY, CHOPPED FINELY

½ TEASPOON DRIED BASIL

½ TEASPOON DRIED THYME

½ TEASPOON GROUND CINNAMON

1 TEASPOON SALT

2 DASHES OF TABASCO SAUCE

½ TABLESPOON WORCESTERSHIRE SAUCE

300 ml (½ PINT) WATER

450 ml (¾ PINT) TOMATO KETCHUP

6 TABLESPOONS RED OR WHITE WINE VINEGAR

1 TABLESPOON 'LIQUID SMOKE' (OPTIONAL)

JUICE OF 1 LEMON

1 TEASPOON GRATED LEMON ZEST

Heat the oil in a large heavy-based saucepan and add the garlic, green peppers, onions and celery. Cook, over medium heat, for about 5 minutes, stirring frequently. Add all the remaining ingredients, except the lemon juice and zest, and cook for a further 5 minutes or so.

Add the lemon juice and zest and simmer, over gentle heat, for about 30–40 minutes, stirring occasionally towards the end of cooking. Add a little more water if the sauce is too thick.

Serve with chicken, pork, beef or fish.

Rich Chinese sauce

MAKES ABOUT 450 ml (¾ PINT)

6 TABLESPOONS SOY SAUCE

4 TABLESPOONS CLEAR HONEY

1 TABLESPOON SOFT BROWN SUGAR

½ TEASPOON CURRY POWDER

½ TEASPOON GROUND GINGER

1 LARGE GARLIC CLOVE, CRUSHED

½ TEASPOON SALT

A PINCH OF FRESHLY GROUND BLACK PEPPER

3 TABLESPOONS PRESERVED GINGER, DRAINED WELL AND CHOPPED FINELY

6 TABLESPOONS DRY OR MEDIUM DRY SHERRY OR WHITE WINE

Combine the soy sauce, honey, sugar, curry powder, ground ginger, garlic, salt and pepper in a heavy-based saucepan and, over gentle heat, bring it to the boil, stirring continuously.

Draw the pan to one side and stir in the preserved ginger and the sherry or wine. Reduce the heat and simmer for 5–10 minutes, stirring until the sauce thickens.

Serve with chicken, pork or beef.

Honey and mustard sauce

MAKES ABOUT 250 ml (8 fl oz)

6 TABLESPOONS CLEAR HONEY

3 TABLESPOONS ENGLISH OR FRENCH MUSTARD

½ TEASPOON HORSERADISH SAUCE

1 TABLESPOON CORNFLOUR

3 TABLESPOONS RED WINE VINEGAR

2 TABLESPOONS LEMON JUICE

Put all the ingredients in a heavy-based saucepan and cook over gentle heat, stirring continuously, until the mixture clears and thickens slightly.

Serve with hamburgers, steaks and chops.

Indonesian sauce

MAKES ABOUT 300 ml (½ PINT)

1 TABLESPOON OIL

4 TABLESPOONS SMOOTH PEANUT BUTTER

150 ml (¼ PINT) TOMATO KETCHUP

3 TABLESPOONS WORCESTERSHIRE SAUCE

GARLIC POWDER TO TASTE

¼ TEASPOON SALT

Heat the oil in a heavy-based saucepan and add the peanut butter. Cook over gentle heat, stirring occasionally, until the peanut butter thickens and darkens slightly. Remove the pan from the heat immediately and stir in the tomato ketchup and Worcestershire sauce.

Season the sauce to taste with garlic powder and the salt. Allow to stand for 2 hours before use.

Reheat the sauce gently and add a little water if the sauce is too thick.

Serve with chicken and steaks. It can also be used to baste chicken.

Soy, orange and wine sauce

MAKES ABOUT 450 ml (¾ PINT)

4 TABLESPOONS SOY SAUCE

6 TABLESPOONS ORANGE JUICE

6 TABLESPOONS SOFT BROWN SUGAR

150 ml (¼ PINT) DRY WHITE WINE

½ TEASPOON MUSTARD POWDER

½ TEASPOON GROUND GINGER

2 DASHES OF TABASCO SAUCE

2 SHALLOTS, CHOPPED FINELY

A PINCH OF GROUND CINNAMON

3 TABLESPOONS WATER

2 TEASPOONS CORNFLOUR

SALT AND FRESHLY GROUND BLACK PEPPER

Combine all the ingredients, except the cornflour and seasoning, in a heavy-based saucepan and bring slowly to the boil, stirring continuously. Allow to simmer for about 5 minutes. Stir in the cornflour to thicken. Season to taste with salt and pepper.

Serve with chicken and pork.

Jim's jammy-ginger sauce

MAKES ABOUT 350 ml (12 fl oz)

500 g (1 lb) APRICOT JAM

4 TABLESPOONS DRY WHITE WINE OR WHITE WINE VINEGAR

2 TABLESPOONS MELTED BUTTER OR OIL

1 TABLESPOON FRESHLY GRATED ROOT GINGER OR ½ TEASPOON GROUND GINGER

½ TEASPOON SALT

Combine all the ingredients in a heavy-based saucepan and heat until simmering, stirring occasionally.

Serve with chicken and pork.

Flavoured butters

Providing guests with a selection of barbecue sauces with which to baste their food could be time consuming and fairly expensive. Offering them an assortment of flavoured butters is less so. For those who haven't time to prepare the butters, there is a modest range of basic flavours, such as herbs and garlic, black pepper and blue cheese, available in small packets from most supermarkets.

However, flavoured butter can be made up seven to ten days before use as long as it is kept in the refrigerator in a covered dish. Remove the flavoured butter from the refrigerator and then melt and brush it on to the food; or place a piece of the butter on the second side of the meat during the final two minutes of cooking and allow it to melt. Some of the butters also make tasty and reasonably economical sandwich spreads.

To prepare the following butters, beat the butter until soft; then add and thoroughly mix in the other ingredients. Using wet hands, shape into a roll about 4 cm (1½ inches) in diameter. Wrap gently in foil and chill well. Keep in the refrigerator until ready to serve.

MUSTARD AND ONION BUTTER
2 TABLESPOONS DIJON MUSTARD
1 TABLESPOON FINELY CHOPPED SPRING ONION
1 GARLIC CLOVE, CHOPPED VERY FINELY
¼ TEASPOON FRESHLY GROUND BLACK PEPPER
A DASH OF WORCESTERSHIRE SAUCE
125 g (4 oz) BUTTER

Use with red meat and duck.

GARLIC BUTTER (MEDIUM STRENGTH)
1 GARLIC CLOVE, CHOPPED VERY FINELY
1½ TABLESPOONS CHOPPED FRESH PARSLEY
125 g (4 oz) BUTTER

Use with seafood, red meat, vegetables and french bread.

BLUE CHEESE BUTTER
75 g (3 oz) BLUE CHEESE, CRUMBLED FINELY
¼ TEASPOON PAPRIKA
1 GARLIC CLOVE, CHOPPED VERY FINELY
1 TABLESPOON FINELY CHOPPED SPRING ONION
125 g (4 oz) BUTTER

Use with red meat (including hamburgers). It also makes an excellent filling for baked potatoes.

HERB AND GARLIC BUTTER
½ TEASPOON DRIED TARRAGON OR ROSEMARY
1 TABLESPOON FINELY CHOPPED FRESH CHIVES
1 TABLESPOON FINELY CHOPPED FRESH PARSLEY
1 GARLIC CLOVE, CHOPPED VERY FINELY
¼ TEASPOON SALT
A PINCH OF FRESHLY GROUND BLACK PEPPER
125 g (4 oz) BUTTER

Use with poultry, seafood, vegetables and french bread.

MAÎTRE D'HÔTEL BUTTER
2 TEASPOONS FINELY CHOPPED FRESH PARSLEY
¼ TEASPOON SALT
2 TEASPOONS LEMON JUICE
¼ TEASPOON DRIED THYME
A PINCH OF FRESHLY GROUND BLACK PEPPER
125 g (4 oz) BUTTER

Use with vegetables and fish, or as a baste for chicken.

LEMON AND PARSLEY BUTTER
2 TABLESPOONS LEMON JUICE
1 TEASPOON FINELY GRATED LEMON ZEST
1 TABLESPOON DRY WHITE WINE (OPTIONAL)
1 TABLESPOON FINELY CHOPPED FRESH PARSLEY
125 g (4 oz) BUTTER

Use with seafood, poultry and vegetables.

ORANGE AND HONEY BUTTER
1 TABLESPOON ORANGE JUICE
1 TABLESPOON FINELY GRATED ORANGE ZEST
1 TABLESPOON CLEAR HONEY
2 TEASPOONS FINELY CHOPPED FRESH PARSLEY
125 g (4 oz) BUTTER

Use with lamb, duck, chicken and turkey.

TARRAGON AND PARSLEY BUTTER
¼ TEASPOON DRIED CRUSHED TARRAGON
1 TABLESPOON FINELY CHOPPED FRESH PARSLEY
½ TEASPOON GRATED LEMON ZEST
2 TEASPOONS LEMON JUICE
¼ TEASPOON SALT
125 g (4 oz) BUTTER

Use with red meat, especially steaks.

Seasonings

Obvious though it may sound, flavour is a matter of taste. So personal preference will always dictate how much, or how little, boost is given to a food's natural smell or taste by the addition of seasonings. The judicious use of carefully selected spices and herbs, or one of the excellent commercial seasonings, will improve marginally (anything more would be counter-productive) the appearance, flavour and aroma of a food. There are, of course, exceptions, and one that springs to mind is Tandoori Chicken (page 82), which is made with a number of spices.

Spice-based seasonings, made from dried and ground aromatic roots, bark, seeds, etc. require a light touch. On the other hand, herbs from the more temperate regions of the world can be used, generally speaking, in spoonfuls rather than 'pinches'; handfuls can be used to produce fragrant smoke.

Herbs can be enjoyed by both inside and outside cooks, so it makes sense to cultivate a small herb garden between kitchen door and barbecue area. For those without a garden, the more manageable herbs, such as thyme, marjoram and tarragon, can be grown in a window box or tub. Rosemary has remained my favourite herb over the years, not only because of its bewitching aroma, but also because of its versatility: mature branches of the herb, stripped of all but the end leaves, make exotic skewers for lamb and beef kebabs.

Use the seasonings in the following chart according to personal taste or as directed on the product labelling. The quantities given are as a guide only for four servings.

HERBS AND SPICES	DESCRIPTION	QUANTITY	MEAT	POULTRY	FISH	MISCELLANEOUS
Allspice	nutmeg, cinnamon and cloves	¼–½ teaspoon	ground: all meat, especially beef and pork; curries whole: pot roasts	ground: all poultry	ground: all fish	ground: barbecue sauces whole: marinades
Basil	sweet, mild aniseed flavour	½–1 teaspoon	all meat, especially beef; mince and casseroles cooked with tomatoes and garlic	all poultry; casseroles	all fish	all vegetables, especially tomatoes; pizzas; marinades; salad dressings
Bay leaves	delicately sweet and fragrant flavour	1 leaf or ¼ teaspoon	ground: all meat; casseroles; mince whole: as above; roasts	ground: all poultry whole: all poultry	ground: all fish whole: all fish	ground: sauces; stocks; marinades
Cardamom	rich, sweet, lemony, eucalyptus flavour	¼–½ teaspoon crushed seed	ground: all meat, especially lamb; curries	ground: all poultry; curries; casseroles		ground: marinades
Celery seed	pleasantly bitter, fresh celery taste	¼–½ teaspoon	all meat; casseroles	all poultry	all fish	all vegetables, especially carrots and cauliflower; sauces; marinades
Chillies	fiery hot	*use with caution*	crushed and whole: all meat; casseroles; curries; chili-con-carne	crushed and whole: all poultry; casseroles		'devilled' sauces; marinades, Indian and Mexican cooking
Chives	mild onion flavour	1 teaspoon– 1 tablespoon	all meat	all poultry; casseroles	all fish	sauces; as a garnish
Cinnamon	strong, sweet and spicy flavour	¼–½ teaspoon 1 stick	ground: all meat; casseroles; curries sticks: pot roasts; curries	ground: all poultry; curries	ground: all fish; curries	ground: sweet and sour barbecue sauces sticks: mulled wine
Cloves	strong, sweet and aromatic flavour	¼–½ teaspoon 1 or 2 whole	ground: all meat; casseroles; curries whole: studded ham or pork	ground: all poultry	ground: all fish	whole: marinades

HERBS AND SPICES	DESCRIPTION	QUANTITY	MEAT	POULTRY	FISH	MISCELLANEOUS
Coriander seed	sweet, spicy orange flavour	½–1 teaspoon	ground: all meat, especially lamb and pork; curries whole: pot roasts	ground: all poultry; curries	ground: all fish	ground: all rice and pasta dishes; root vegetables, especially carrots
Cumin	strong, pungent 'Eastern' flavour	¼–½ teaspoon	ground: all meat, especially lamb; kebabs	ground: all poultry; casseroles; curries		ground: Indian and Mexican cooking; carrots; cabbage
Curry powder	available in varying strengths to suit taste	1–2 tablespoons	all meat; curries; casseroles; roasts; grills	all poultry; curries; casseroles	all fish; grills; curries	Indian cooking; marinades; sauces
Dill seed	aromatic, mild aniseed flavour	¼–½ teaspoon	all meat, especially lamb and pork; casseroles	some chicken casseroles	some baked fish	dressings; cabbage; potatoes; coleslaw
Dill weed	mild, slight aniseed flavour	¼–½ teaspoon	all meat, especially pork, veal, lamb and ham	all poultry; casseroles; pies	all fish, especially seafood, cod and tuna	sauces; dressings; salads; vegetables, especially cucumber, carrots and potatoes
Fennel seed	mild, sweet liquorice flavour	¼–½ teaspoon	all meat, especially pork; curries	all poultry; casseroles; curries	all fish, especially mackerel, tuna and herring	Indian cooking; apple dishes
Garam masala	aromatic, curry spices	1–2 teaspoons (add at end of cooking)	all curried meat dishes; grills; kebabs; roasts	all curried poultry	all curried fish	curried sauces; marinades
Garlic (minced, granules, salt)	pungent, 'the taste of France'	¼ teaspoon = 1 fresh garlic clove	all meat; casseroles; roasts	all poultry; roasts; casseroles	all fish	garlic bread; sauces; marinades; vegetables, especially tomatoes, courgettes and beans

HERBS AND SPICES	DESCRIPTION	QUANTITY	MEAT	POULTRY	FISH	MISCELLANEOUS
Ginger	hot, sweet and spicy, with a lemony taste	¼–½ teaspoon	ground: all meat, especially beef, pork and ham; curries	ground: some chicken casseroles; curries	ground: grilled fish; some curried dishes	ground: Indian and Chinese cooking; sauces whole: marinades
Herbes de Provence	blend of mild herbs; 'the taste of South of France'	½–1 teaspoon	all meat; casseroles and mince cooked with tomatoes	all poultry; casseroles	all fish	French cooking; marinades; savoury butters; dressings; vegetables, especially tomatoes
Mace	similar to, but slightly stronger than, nutmeg	¼–½ teaspoon 2–3 blades	ground: all meat, especially beef, pork and lamb; curries; sausage-meat	all poultry; casseroles		ground: Indian cooking; spinach; mushrooms blade: marinades
Marjoram	sweet, fragrant, similar to, but milder than, oregano	½–1 teaspoon	all meat, especially beef, lamb, pork, ham and sausagemeat	all poultry; casseroles	all fish, especially seafood, cod and tuna	all vegetables, especially tomatoes; salads; savoury butters; pizzas; sauces
Mint	fresh, spearmint taste	½–1 tablespoon	lamb dishes, especially casseroles and roasts	some casseroles	some fish	marinades; vegetables, especially peas, potatoes and tomatoes; mint sauce
Mixed herbs	mix of mild, sweet herbs	½–1 teaspoon	all meat; casseroles; mince	all poultry; casseroles	all fish	all vegetables, especially tomatoes; savoury butters; salads
Mixed spice	blend of sweet spices	½–1 teaspoon	all meat, especially beef, lamb and pork; minces	all chicken casseroles; 'sweet and sour' dishes	some fish	root vegetables
Mustard seed	sharp and pungent	¼–½ teaspoon	all meat, especially steaks; casseroles; pot roasts	all poultry; casseroles	some baked fish	marinades; some sauces; vegetables; dressings

HERBS AND SPICES	DESCRIPTION	QUANTITY	MEAT	POULTRY	FISH	MISCELLANEOUS
Nutmeg	sweet, mild and spicy	pinch – ¼ teaspoon	all meat, especially lamb; curries; sausagemeat	all poultry; curries; casseroles	some fish	sauces; vegetables, especially spinach and potatoes
Onion (minced, salt, powder)	familiar sweet and pungent smell	use to taste	all meat, to replace fresh onions	all poultry	all fish	marinades
Oregano	strong, with a characteristic Italian flavour	½–1 teaspoon	all meat; casseroles; lasagne; spaghetti bolognaise	all poultry; casseroles	some fish, especially cod	pizzas; marinades; Italian cooking; vegetables, especially tomatoes
Paprika	mild and sweet with attractive red-orange colour	pinch– 2 tablespoons	all meat, especially pork and ham	all poultry	all fish; garnish for seafood	Spanish cooking; paprika butter; garnish for vegetables
Hot paprika	rich, piquant, earthy with a slightly hot flavour	1–2 tablespoons	all meat; goulash; casseroles	all poultry; casseroles	all fish	Hungarian cooking; garnish for vegetables; salads
Parsley	mild and fresh flavour	use freely	all meat; mince; casseroles; pies	all poultry; casseroles; pies	all fish	sauces; savoury butters; dressings; salads; garnish for vegetables
Peppercorns, white and black	white are less pungent than black	to taste	ground: all meat; grills; casseroles	ground: all poultry	ground: all fish	whole: marinades
Peppercorns, green	clean, fresh, piquant flavour	½–1 teaspoon	all meat, especially pork and beef; steaks; casseroles; roasts	all poultry; casseroles	some fish	crush, grind or use whole for marinades and sauces; garnish for vegetables
Pepper, cayenne	hot and fiery	add a pinch at a time, with caution	all meat; curries; casseroles; 'devilled' dishes	all poultry; casseroles; curries	some curried dishes	Indian cooking; sauces; garnish for vegetables

HERBS AND SPICES	DESCRIPTION	QUANTITY	MEAT	POULTRY	FISH	MISCELLANEOUS
Poppy seed	mild, nutty flavour	¼–½ teaspoon	all curry dishes; garnish for casseroles and pie-crusts	some poultry for garnish	some fish for garnish	garnish for vegetables
Rosemary	delicately sweet and fragrant	½–1 teaspoon	all meat, especially lamb; roasts; casseroles	all poultry; roasts; casseroles	all fish	pizzas; marinades; savoury butters; vegetables, especially cauliflower, beans, potatoes and tomatoes
Saffron	delicate, honey-like; beautiful yellow colour	use several strands	pork and lamb; curries	all poultry	some fish, especially seafood; paella	all rice dishes; curried vegetables
Sage	bold, penetrating flavour	½–1 teaspoon	all meat, especially pork, ham and bacon; casseroles; roasts; grills; sausagemeat	all poultry; roasts; casseroles	some fish, especially cod	marinades; vegetables, especially onion and tomatoes
Sesame seed	nutty flavour	½–1 teaspoon	garnish for pie-crusts, casseroles and curries	some poultry, especially for coatings	some fish, especially for coatings	Chinese cooking; salads; vegetarian dishes; garnish for vegetables
Tarragon	strong and distinctive fresh aniseed flavour	½–1 teaspoon	all meat, especially lamb and pork; roasts; casseroles; grills	all poultry; roasts; casseroles; fricassees	all fish, especially cod, tuna and mackerel	marinades; savoury butters; vegetables, especially tomatoes and carrots
Thyme	strong, pleasantly fragrant	½–1 teaspoon	all meat, especially beef and pork; mince; casseroles; sausagemeat	all poultry; roasts; casseroles	all fish, especially cod	marinades; savoury butters; all vegetables, especially carrots and tomatoes
Turmeric	strong, pleasantly bitter with a rich golden colour	½–1 teaspoon	all meat; curries	all pale chicken dishes; curries	curries	curried vegetables; Indian cooking

Cooking time charts

Roasting (using indirect heat)

FOOD	CUT	DEGREE OF COOKING	HEAT SETTING	INTERNAL TEMPERATURE	APPROXIMATE MINUTES PER 500 g (1 lb)
Beef	rib-roast	rare	low/medium	75°C/140°F	18–20
		medium	low/medium	85°C/160°F	20–25
		well-done	low/medium	90°C/170°F	25–30
	sirloin		medium	75–90°C/140–170°F	25–30
	rump/rolled		medium	80–90°C/150–170°F	25–30
Lamb	leg	rare	medium	75°C/140°F	18–22
		medium	medium	85°C/160°F	22–28
		well-done	medium	90°C/170°F	28–33
	crown roast	rare	medium	75°C/140°F	25–30
		medium	medium	85°C/160°F	30–36
		well-done	medium	90°C/170°F	36–42
	shoulder	medium	medium	85°C/160°F	22–28
		well-done	medium	90°C/170°F	28–33
Pork	loin	well-done	low/medium	100°C/185°F	25–30
	fresh ham	well-done	low/medium	100°C/185°F	20–25
	crown	well-done	low/medium	100°C/185°F	25–35
Veal	loin	well-done	low/medium	100°C/185°F	20–25
	leg	well-done	low/medium	100°C/185°F	20–25
	shoulder	well-done	low/medium	100°C/185°F	20–25
Poultry	chicken	well-done	low/medium	100°C/185°F	15–20
	turkey	well-done	low/medium	100°C/185°F	12–20*
	duckling	well-done	low/medium	100°C/185°F	15–20

*cooking times will vary considerably according to the weight of the bird

Grilling

| FOOD | CUT | SIZE OR WEIGHT | HEAT SETTING | APPROXIMATE COOKING TIME (EACH SIDE) IN MINUTES | | |
				RARE	MEDIUM	WELL-DONE
Beef	steak	2.5 cm (1 inch)	high	3–4	4–5	5–6
	steak	4 cm (1½ inches)	high	5–6	7–8	9–10
	steak*	5 cm (2 inches)	high	7–8	9–10	10–11
	flank steak	whole	high	3–4+		
	hamburger	2.5 cm (1 inch)	medium/high	3–4	5–6	6–8
Lamb	chops	2.5 cm (1 inch)	medium/high	5–6	7–8	9–10
	liver**	1 cm (½ inch)	medium/high		5–6	
Pork	chops	2.5 cm (1 inch)	medium/high			15–18
	spare ribs	whole or section	medium			55–75
	liver**	1 cm (½ inch)	medium/high		6–7	
	ham	2.5 cm (1 inch)	medium			15–20
Poultry	chicken	1.5 kg (3½ lb)				
	split		medium			35–45
	duck	1.75 kg (4 lb)				
	split		medium	5–6	10–12	25–28
Veal	steaks					
	or chops	2.5 cm (1 inch)	medium			9–12
Fish	steak	1 cm (½ inch)	medium			2–3
	steak	2.5 cm (1 inch)	medium			5
Lobster	split	500–750 g				
		(1–1½ lb)	medium/high			7–10

*If the steak is 5 cm (2 inches) or more thick you can use a meat thermometer to judge – steak is rare at 70°C/130°F, well-done at 90°C/170°F

†Maximum cooking time for the steak to remain tender

**Avoid overcooking or the liver will become tough

Spit roasting

FOOD	CUT	SIZE OR WEIGHT	HEAT SETTING	APPROXIMATE COOKING TIME IN HOURS*		
				RARE	MEDIUM	WELL-DONE
				75°C/140°F	85°C/160°F	90°C/170°F
Beef	rump	1.25–2.25 kg (3–5 lb)	medium	1½–2	2¼–3	3–4
	sirloin	2.25–2.75 kg (5–6 lb)	medium/high	1¼–1¾	2¼–3	3–4
	rolled rib	1.75–2.75 kg (4–6 lb)	medium/high	2–2½	2¼–3	3¼–4½
Lamb	leg	1.5–3.5 kg (3½–8 lb)	medium	1–1¼	1½–2	2–3¼
	rolled shoulder	1.25–2.75 kg (3–6 lb)	medium	1–1¼	1½–2	2–3¼
						100°C/185°F
Pork	shoulder	1.25–2.75 kg (3–6 lb)	medium/high			2–3
	loin	1.25–2.25 kg (3–5 lb)	medium/high			2–3
	spare ribs	1–1.75 kg (2–4 lb)	medium/high			1–1¾
	fresh ham	2.25–3.5 kg (5–8 lb)	medium			3½–4½
Poultry	chicken	1.1–2.25 kg (2½–5 lb)	medium			1–1½
	turkey	3.5–7 kg (8–16 lb)	medium			2–4
	duckling	1.75–2.75 kg (4–6 lb)	medium			1–2
Veal	leg	2.25–3.5 kg (5–8 lb)	medium			2–3
	rolled shoulder	1.25–2.25 kg (3–5 lb)	medium			1½–2½
	loin	2.25–2.75 kg (5–6 lb)	medium			1½–2¼
						65–70°C/120–130°F
Fish	large, whole	2.25–4.5 kg (5–10 lb)	low/medium			1–1¼
	small, whole	750 g–1.75 kg (1½–4 lb)	low/medium			½–1

*For accuracy use a meat thermometer and cook to the internal temperatures given in the chart

American and Australian conversion chart

Apart from the usual basic measures, such as
'teaspoon', 'tablespoon' and 'pinch', all the
quantities and measurements in this book
are given in both metric and imperial form.
All spoon measures are level unless
otherwise stated.

	BRITISH	AMERICAN	AUSTRALIAN
Teaspoons and tablespoons	1 teaspoon (5 ml)	1 teaspoon (5 ml)	1 teaspoon (5 ml)
	*1 tablespoon	1 rounded tablespoon	1 scant tablespoon
	2 tablespoons	2 tablespoons	1½ tablespoons
	3 tablespoons	3 tablespoons	2½ tablespoons
	4 tablespoons	4 tablespoons	3½ tablespoons
	5 tablespoons	5 tablespoons	4½ tablespoons
†Cup measures – liquid	4 tablespoons	¼ cup	¼ cup
	125 ml (4 fl oz)	½ cup	½ cup
	250 ml (8 fl oz)	1 cup	1 cup
	450 ml (¾ pint)	2 cups	2 cups
	600 ml (1 pint)	2½ cups	2½ cups
Cup measures – solid	500 g (1 lb) butter	2 cups	2 cups
	200 g (7 oz) long-grain rice	1 cup	1 cup
	500 g (1 lb) granulated sugar	2 cups	2 cups
	50 g (2 oz) chopped onion	½ cup	½ cup
	50 g (2 oz) soft breadcrumbs	1 cup	1 cup
	500 g (1 lb) plain flour	4 cups	4 cups
	50 g (2 oz) thinly sliced mushrooms	½ cup	½ cup

*British standard tablespoon = 15 ml; American standard tablespoon = 14.2 ml; Australian standard tablespoon = 20 ml. (Note: due to the nature of most of the recipes in this book, differences between tablespoon capacities should not have any adverse effect on the taste of the food)
†American measuring cup = 250 ml (8 fl oz); Australian measuring cup = 250 ml (8 fl oz). (Note: British pint = 20 fl oz; American pint = 16 fl oz; Australian pint = 20 fl oz)